Before You Go

Why Planning Your Funeral Makes Sense

Cathy Boomer

Illustrations by Sam Boomer

Mission Point Press

Readers are encouraged to go to www.MissionPointPress.com to contact the author or to find information on how to buy this book in bulk at a discounted rate.

Published by Mission Point Press
2554 Chandler Rd.
Traverse City, MI 49696
(231) 421-9513
www.MissionPointPress.com

Illustrations by Sam Boomer

Book design by Janella Williams

ISBN 978-1-965278-46-8

Library of Congress Control Number: 2025903732

To the ones who believe in me:
Your unwavering faith lifts me up,
Your encouragement fuels my journey,
And your love reminds me that I am never alone.
—cjb

"No one wants to die. Even people who want to go to heaven don't want to die to get there. And yet, death is the destination we all share. No one has ever escaped it, and that is how it should be, because death is very likely the single best invention of life. It's life's change agent. It clears out the old to make way for the new."

—Steve Jobs

TABLE of CONTENTS

Introduction:
- Why Now?

TABLE of CONTENTS

> *"Nothing can happen more beautiful than death."*
>
> · —Walt Whitman

INTRODUCTION
Why Now?

We know we won't live forever... that life can be fragile, and its end can come suddenly. We also know how uncomfortable the thought of death can be, especially our own. Yet it's guaranteed to happen. And too often we don't think ahead about the burden we'll leave our family if we check out unexpectedly. I don't mean a financial burden. I mean the emotional burden of not discussing your wishes prior to your death.

If there's a single message in this book, it's this: It's critical to let your family know now your after-death wishes. Do you want a funeral? Or a memorial service? Or a private, family-only farewell? Cremation? Traditional burial? Do you want your death made public with a written obituary or through social media? Or kept as quiet as possible? If there's a gathering to celebrate your life, what music do you want played, if any? Do you want folks to spend money on flowers, or instead donate those funds to a charity?

Just as important is this question: To what extent do you want your family to decide these questions? Sure, after-death services honor the dead. But aren't these celebrations mainly for the living?

The list of options and issues surrounding death is lengthy. My goal with this book is to help you and your family navigate through them. But do so in a welcoming and friendly way.

"I don't believe in dying. It's been done. I'm working on a new exit. Besides, I can't die now—I'm booked," said entertainer George Burns. Burns was such a believer in not passing that he waited until just a few months after celebrating his 100th birthday to do so. Sadly, not all of us will reach such a milestone, but using this book to thoughtfully plan for your passing honors you, and your family, with peace of mind.

The Importance of Planning Your Funeral

Unlike nearly every other consumer retail experience, the funeral service experience hasn't really changed in seventy-five years. There was a time, you would take a trip to the hardware store and ask the man behind the counter to help you match a nut with a bolt. The clerk would walk you down the nuts-and-bolts aisle looking for the correct bolt. The purchase was made, and the shopping experience was finished. This is how the funeral buying experience still works. You walk into the funeral home and the funeral director typically manages every step of the process.

Over the last twenty years most consumer experiences include reviews, likes, and word-of-mouth referrals. Whether we walk into a store or do research online, shopping has become a sport. Salesclerks are few and far between and online chat offers limited insight into the product. Yet, people continue to die, and the industry has not kept up with current consumer expectations.

Exhausted, sleep deprived, and gripped in sadness at our worst moment of loss, we must go to a building that we've never been in before, trust a stranger with our most important decisions and make a sizeable financial investment. The funeral industry has a terrible reputation of taking advantage of people. Are they going to take advantage of me?

The selection of the funeral home could have been influenced by family members who recognize the name as familiar because they've driven by it for thirty years. We don't know very much about the process, the company, or their pricing. As of this printing only 25% of funeral homes have pricing displayed on their website. This adds to the mystery. When the time comes, you often walk in blind to the cost as well as the countless decisions that need to be made in quick succession. What other purchase do you make for that amount of money without researching it ahead of time besides funeral services?

Many are familiar with pre-paid funeral plans; I advocate for education around the entire process to learn what to expect with local funeral service providers. Informed consumers can budget for and even pre-pay funeral and burial services. This can only be done by understanding the associated costs.

One of the challenges is our culture tends to not discuss the end of life. Therefore, many consumers are not educated on the workings of the funeral industry. This puts families at a disadvantage when they begin this journey and emphasizes the importance of letting families prepare in advance. The more you know, the more you can communicate your personal preferences to your next of kin, best friend, or family members. Writing down those wishes is a gift, your final gift to them, freeing them from the burden of guessing. *Before You Go* will build your knowledge base and help to clarify your preferences for your family and empower them to move forward.

If Not You, Then Whom?

Families want to align with your wishes. I once met with a family, a husband and his two daughters. Their wife and mother died suddenly. They clearly cherished this woman with their whole hearts. It poured from every word they spoke. Often the first question in planning is to identify their wish for cremation or traditional services. In this family, the husband and one daughter said her wish would be cremation. The second daughter said no, she wanted traditional burial and brought in a dress that her mother had given her with a note on it, in her mother's handwriting that said, "Bury me in this dress." The family had the guidance they needed, and their decision was made and the conflict was resolved. The mother's handwriting supported her wishes. It's rare to have something so concrete. Now is the time for you to give your family the equivalent of this handwritten note. Your service or memorial may be more sacred than some family members are comfortable with. It may be more secular than some family members are comfortable with. There is no right or wrong. This is your direction which will hopefully prevail over any squabbles or different opinions.

Writing down our wishes or gathering with friends to discuss how you envision your funeral and leaving documentation needs to move into the mainstream of the consumer mindset. There was a time when no one talked about S.E.X. Not on TV, maybe a little bit in the movies. It was considered taboo. Death is a topic that's still taboo. Especially if you're over a certain age. Any younger, it may not be a topic that many people have faced. The "older generation" have been comfortable leaving this in the hands of their children. Since we don't want to think about losing our loved ones and funerals are not routinely discussed, family members may have no idea what you'd want to have in place. It's a wonder that funerals get planned at all!

Take a minute, by yourself or with friends or family—and get started on planning your funeral. Take an hour or two and start the conversation and begin to write down your wishes. Schedule a small gathering to plan your funeral. It will be easier when there are several friends or family doing the same thing. Mention this as an idea for a pre- or post-holiday activity. When you bring up the subject or approach it with your family or friends, they may not want to discuss it. If so, you can tell them that you're going ahead and leaving them some direction, for when the time comes. It will make the topic easier because they'll know that you're thinking ahead to make it easier for them.

This is a process that takes time and might have several steps to get family input or explore any family plots or traditions. You may simply want to think about it. The goal is to make your wishes known. That is done by initiating the conversation in a safe setting and exchanging thoughts and ideas with your family or friends.

Thoughts and ideas are one thing. Capturing that information and getting it down on paper in some manner to leave behind for your family, that's a gift. How and what to do in the unlikely situation, ok, 100% likely, that you'll die? What should they do? What would you want them to do? How do they go about doing it? What's important and what's not important? Give them permission, information, and direction to fulfill your last wishes.

The essence of *Before You Go* is to facilitate the conversation and any action needed to capture your wishes. This can be accomplished with other people that want to do the same or you can do it on your own. There are pages at the end of each chapter to capture your thoughts and begin the planning. Be sure and mention to family and friends that you have left your wishes in the book. The following chapters cover all aspects of funeral preparation to guide your planning. This can easily be modified or updated as changes occur in your life and your funeral plans may change based on those life changes.

> *"To the well-organized mind, death is but the next adventure."*
> —Dumbledore

CHAPTER 1
First Things First

Where do we start? What do we do first? Each decision builds on the next. The first question is almost always would you or your family prefer a traditional burial or cremation?

The closely followed second question is do you want a service? What does that look like: a traditional service, celebration of life, or a graveside service? What would my family want? This is only the beginning of the options for consideration.

Funeral planning is like other aspects of our lives—begin with the end in mind. How do we celebrate someone who was important in our lives? What elements of the funeral will magnify the love and admiration and leave a positive imprint for our loved one? What makes a funeral memorable?

It's difficult to personalize a funeral for someone after meeting with a funeral director for one to two hours. Seasoned funeral directors should begin with one question, "Tell me about your loved one?"

That question and the answers that follow will guide the whole process. If they loved the outdoors, that could inform decisions about flowers. If they felt strongly about being cremated, that will guide the service decisions. If they had a lot of friends or were younger, that will direct practical venue suggestions. If they had a church home or were agnostic, that information guides the path for a service and celebration that will exemplify their life.

Using that question as a guiding principle, "Tell me about your loved one?" Leads to other personal questions.

When my son was 20, he was in an Air Force ROTC program and planning on a career in the military. He participated in a summer program that included a parachute jump out of airplanes. That's something that I had always wanted to do. I was excited for him. However, beyond the excitement, I knew it would be wise to plan for the worst-case scenario. What if the chute didn't open?

I went into his room and told him, "Ok we're going to plan your funeral in case the worst thing happens." He told me I was crazy, but I forged ahead. We began with what was his wish, traditional or cremation?

That prompted him to ask me what my preference would be for myself. After discussing the pros and cons of each, we then went to other details like flowers, music, and where he'd like to be buried. He had some very specific requests. He wanted wildflowers for flowers, music from Johnny Cash, and not to be buried at a big cemetery by a busy intersection. The conversation evolved and included his favorite books and movies. He asked if I wanted to know his favorite quotes. (I didn't even know he had favorite quotes!) As we continued, he shared his favorite memories and the things he liked most that we did as a family. With that conversation, I learned things about him that I did not know. It was a fruitful conversation, for those reasons alone. At the end of this discussion, I was half laughing and half crying. He was completely laughing at me, but if the worst thing had happened, I would have known what to do.

Understanding

As you think about your loved one, do you know their wishes for traditional burial or cremation? Reflect on past conversations. For example, "I never want to be cremated" or "I don't want to be in the family plot with Aunt Sue." Sometimes people change their mind or remember things differently than how they occurred. No single decision has to define all the next steps, but it's important to consider those stated preferences and move forward with next questions regarding service structures and dates, casket or urn. And whether you are asking those questions or you are asking the questions of yourself, let's look at the two basic options and go from there. Is your wish for:

- Cremation?
- Traditional Burial?

Cremation

In recent years cremation is increasing in popularity across the country. In the Midwest, cremation accounts for approximately 60% of final plans. On the coasts, the number is slightly higher, up to 75%. A couple of societal factors have influenced this shift from the cost to the transience of the population and even proximity to the family plot.

Cremation costs are approximately 50-80% less than a traditional burial and funeral. The funeral industry's reputation for capitalizing on vulnerabilities of grieving families prompted consumers to become more informed about the funeral planning experience. The family choosing cremation may do so because they want to have fewer decisions to make. That may feel like they have more control over the process. This could be a reason for families' increased decisions for cremation.

With our national/global propensity to move, people often die in a place where they don't necessarily want to be buried. How to transport the body or remains to where they are to be buried can be a little complicated, but it can be done. Globally, a death overseas adds additional challenges from red tape to costs. It's certainly doable with a little patience.

Traditional Burial

The traditional burial service may feel right, because it is what your family has historically done. There may be a family plot available or the comfort that everyone is in the same "neighborhood" in the cemetery.

Whether it's traditional or cremation, it can feel like there is an urgency to hold a service. However, that doesn't have to be the case. Cremation allows for the greatest flexibility and an un-embalmed body will hold for several weeks. Consider your family and set the service dates and times for what works best for them. Perhaps a weekend when family and friends might be freer to travel. Some families wait for better weather or for college breaks. Even look at a special birthday or anniversary date for the celebration. One idea might be to re-order the usual sequence of services. For example, the graveside service could take place right away, with the memorial service at a more convenient time.

More decisions will follow such as who will lead the service, where will it be held, music, poems, and scripture. These preferences are often revealed through the anchor question of, "Tell me about your loved one?"

The Why of Planning

If these decisions have not been initiated before death, then families sit in the pain, the grief, the unbelievability of this moment with no direction and little practical knowledge of options. The importance of addressing this topic is to make sure your wishes are known and to offer your family guidance. Now most importantly, "Tell me about your loved one?"

What are your thoughts on ...

Cremation?

Traditional burial?

"If there ever comes a day when we can't be together, keep me in your heart, I'll stay there forever."

—A.A. Milne

CHAPTER 2
Paint a Picture and Make It Personal

A funeral will not be remembered for whether a person was cremated or buried with a traditional service. What will be remembered is the warmth and feelings around the experience of a funeral, memorial service, the ritual, celebration, gathering, or event. Whatever you call the gathering, those feelings will come from the picture that was painted of a friend or family member. That's why the logical place to start is with the personal details and then move into the funeral service and body preparation decisions. Start with stepping back and consider the details of the life to be celebrated.

I realized that I loved funerals when I was at my friend Judy's father's funeral. I didn't have the privilege of knowing him but went to support her. I drove an hour and a half to attend the service in Judy's hometown. The entire town turned out. The mix of eulogies and selected scriptures threaded through a traditional church service gave me a solid understanding of her father, what mattered to him, and what others thought of him. I quickly realized how many of his attributes were the very same ones I admired in my friend Judy. I drove home thinking, "I love funerals!" Well, a good funeral is celebrating a life well lived—thoughtful details that help to tell a story. How do you do that? What information do you leave to help your family tell your story? Let's look at the different ways to make the service personal.

Leading the Service

Who would you like to lead the service? In a church, it would be the pastor. If the church has multiple pastors, do you have a preference or favorite pastor that you know well? With a more informal service, sometimes the person leading the service fulfills a master of ceremonies type role. That individual would open and close the service and guide the transitions between music, eulogies, and personal comments. It's important to have one person in charge to ensure the experience goes smoothly. With our transient society, it is very likely that the pastor or Father of the church may not know the deceased. That is why it is even more important to leave behind information that will help them guide the service.

Eulogy

A thoughtful eulogy sets the tone, highlights stories, and provides tributes which often make the occasion unique and meaningful. Think of the services that you've been to that are memorable. Did a eulogy pull it together? Did it make you laugh or cry with the memories of the loved one? Did it highlight their best moments or share their eccentricies? Usually, a story highlighting someone's idiosyncrasies, or their humanness are the stories that best resonate with the audience. As the preparations come together the family often asks a close family member or friend to deliver the eulogy. Occasionally someone may ask if they can share remarks, but the honor of deciding who speaks is up to the family. Some eulogies open the service and set the tone then others close and wrap up the experience. And even sometimes the entire service is several individuals speaking one-by-one covering different parts of the person's life.

A church will have specific guidelines for when, where, and how long a eulogy can be given. Sometimes a church will not allow a eulogy in the order of a funeral service. The only time to give remarks may be prior to the start or close of a service, or at a luncheon or reception afterwards. If so, make sure previously discussed details are considered, like having one person to help with the transition of speakers as well as having a microphone available. Even if the memorial celebration is in an informal space, there is nothing worse than not being able to hear the people speaking. Especially if it's outside, it's important to have a microphone available.

The ideal length of a eulogy is four to five minutes. Managing the length is an important part of the process. If it stretches beyond that, people start to get uncomfortable. If it's engaging or funny and full of happy memories about the deceased, it can go on a little longer. However, who gets to determine if it's engaging, funny, and full of happy memories? Sometimes the person who delivers the eulogy is not the best judge.

Recently, I was at a funeral and the woman giving the eulogy talked for fifteen to twenty minutes about their families camping together. It quickly became painfully drawn out. The eulogy isn't meant to be an obituary. It's not a detailed recap of the life events of their friend. It's a time to reflect and highlight a beloved part of a person's life. That can be told with a story or a recap of a time in their life. You might ask two to three people to speak about different parts of their life. For example, childhood, early adult years, family life, professional highlights. For the speaker, it will go by fast. If you're in the audience, it can seem like forever. Opening a microphone at the reception is a way to invite others to tell their favorite stories. Like a wedding toast, some stories are best left for private conversation. As a reminder, the audience will likely include kids, parents, and grandchildren. Make sure the stories and reflections are appropriate for all people attending.

If you have a more informal service or reception planned where remarks will be given, consider including that in the obituary. For example, "the family will host an open house visitation from 3-5 p.m. with special remarks at 4 p.m." People aren't happy if they show up at 4:30 p.m. and hear from the other attendees, "Oh you should have heard her children's eulogy or comments." This way people can attend if it's important to them and if their schedule allows.

With all of this in mind ... who do you want to deliver your eulogy?

Poems/Prayers/Scripture

Any direction you can provide to your family or pastor is helpful. Do you have a favorite story, poem, or prayer that reflects your philosophy on life? It's often a letdown when an officiant just reads the obituary as part of the message for the family and friends. Therefore, if you don't leave personal direction/insights/favorite things, it's up to your family to convey all the information about you. Many families do a great job. Use this opportunity to tell or remind them of your favorite scripture, poem, prayer, books that convey something that you value and are ultimately an essence of what's meaningful to you. If it's a sacred service, this provides insight into your journey as a child of God. If it's a secular service, this can share the light you've brought to the world.

Music

Music sets a powerful tone for the service. Some churches don't allow secular music—a workaround might be to include your favorite music choices in a slideshow if it can't be part of a church service.

When planning a church service, would you prefer traditional or contemporary music? In the Catholic Church, there may be a song that brought you or your family peace from another funeral from the church's suggested funeral song list. A choir member might want the choir to sing at the service. A bell choir member might request the bell choir to be present.

In an alternative setting for a funeral or memorial service, what is the appropriate music for that venue? For those who love new music, a music venue might have the music of an up-and-coming artist playing their favorite songs. While this isn't a concert, having music parsed between a reading of a poem, a eulogy, a message, and favorite stories, can illuminate their love of music and creativity.

If it's music at a more traditional service that you'd like someone to perform, identify that person and your song or songs of choice. The magic number is three. Those songs can be performed as part of a procession/introduction or recession/closing, with maybe one in the middle. If you'd like sacred music, it's also important to leave your favorite hymns or even arrangements to use within the church. Churches may have requirements about who can use their piano or organ or even perform in the sanctuary. They may also have a preferred list of vocalists and musicians. Either way, if you do bring in a vocalist, set aside time for rehearsal prior to the service. If you're selecting a vocalist who lives out of town, that can require a few additional steps.

A slideshow is something that will be watched after a service and it's nice to have it accompanied by favorite music. It can be popular music or favorite tunes, tied to someone's age/music by decade or favorite artist. It's so helpful to leave music choices, so maybe go ahead and leave an .mp3 link. For example, Somewhere Over the Rainbow may be your favorite song, but do you prefer the Judy Garland version or some of the newer interpretations of that song?

Flowers

Flowers sound easy but it's important to have direction. Asking, "What is your loved one's favorite flower, favorite color?" can often elicit a blank stare. Often, it's the stress of the day, but that's why it's important to have some direction. Did they like to garden? What did they plant? Did they like the outdoors or like to hunt? Did they have a favorite color that could be used when making plans for the floral spray or arrangements? What's the season . . . spring, summer, fall, winter? Could the flowers represent their state? For example, Kansas is synonymous with sunflowers. We helped the family of a child who loved Snow White to select meaningful flowers. We worked with the florist who brilliantly incorporated blue birds and a crown. For an ornithologist the florist included a few of the woman's own bird ornaments that she used to decorate her Christmas tree, in the casket spray.

Traditional Burial Flowers

Families often include flowers for a casket spray. They can arrange to have flowers cover the entire casket, especially if the casket lid will be closed for the whole service. If a viewing is held, then typically, the florist prepares a half casket spray. That allows for the lid of the upper half of the casket to be open while the flowers cover the bottom half of the casket. Families have had a casket-length cross of flowers on top of their casket, or a flag with the emblem of their family's heritage. Of course, with a military burial, the American flag will or can cover the casket. Sometimes, the family chooses not to have a casket spray. Instead, a photo of the loved one can reside on top of the casket or next to it on an easel.

Memorial Service Flowers
Without a casket present, there are several options for flowers at the church or venue. With an urn present, a family may choose to have flowers on a table, below the table or next to the table holding the urn. Often a family includes a photo of the loved one up front on a table with any other personal items that tell a life story. Flowers can wrap an urn and be a lovely accent to the urn. Often families place one or two flower arrangements by the altar. They are never placed on the altar table, but another table as a focal point for the service. Sometimes, there are so many flowers given to the family and delivered to the church, that it can be overwhelming. The funeral home or helpers with the service, should be able to catalog the flowers and the people who donated the flowers for you to acknowledge after the service. If it feels too overwhelming to even bring the flowers home or if you don't live in the city of the funeral, you can research organizations that take flowers and repurpose them to donate to nursing homes or hospice houses.

Gravesite Flowers
In the past it was common to take all the flowers from the church to the gravesite to decorate the grave. That has shifted to only taking the flower spray from the casket, to lay on top of the dirt after the grave is filled in. Occasionally, one or two other floral pieces are transported (especially if it's an easel floral display), but typically that's it. Instead, family can take the flowers home to enjoy. It's best to not take glass

containers to a cemetery because of the fear of breakage for the groundskeepers. Family and friends have gone to trouble and money to send you these remembrances and it's nice to have them at home to enjoy.

Often at the end of a graveside service, it's customary to take one or two flowers from the spray home as a remembrance. Because of the ground logistics around the casket at the cemetery, identify one person or the funeral director to retrieve the flowers from the spray. It can be very unsteady ground. Hopefully the cards are still attached, but a good funeral home will have catalogued and somehow documented the flowers so you can acknowledge the sender.

Military veterans often only use a military flag. With or without military honors, the flag can drape the casket in the service and at the graveside. It will be removed and folded prior to burial. Whether the funeral has an open casket or closed, this can serve as a meaningful alternative to flowers.

Catholic funerals place a pall (cloth) over the casket during the church service. Flowers only accompany the casket during the visitation and/or the rosary. The casket spray is removed prior to the Mass of Christian Burial. Following the mass and prior to placing the casket in the funeral coach or hearse, the casket spray is placed back on the casket and then used at the cemetery.

This is good direction to leave for your loved ones.

Picture
That's right! A picture is needed for the program, obituary, and /prayer card. Select a picture when you're in the prime

of your life. If you're the one planning, you get to decide the prime of your life! It's nice to see people in their 20s and 30s, but that might not be how they looked when their younger family members knew them. Anyone recall Glamour Shots? Popular in the 1990s, Glamour Shots were pictures taken in intimate settings with often dramatic hair, makeup, and wardrobe. It might not be best to use such a photo that doesn't even look like you at that age. Fortunately, telephones hold a lot of photos, so it's not hard to find photos of our loved ones. Those might be in a more casual setting than you'd like for the program or obituary photo. A photo by a professional photographer is always helpful because of the quality for reprinting or the digital image. At your next family wedding, consider getting a few professional photos taken that you can use for another occasion, like a funeral. Choose which photo and include it with your funeral plan! If you have identified the funeral home, they should be able to keep it digitally for you in their customer relationship management system. If you print one off, keep it with your funeral plan so it's ready when your family needs it.

Programs

In years past, funeral homes printed and passed out small programs for the occasion. Today there are several additional options.

1. A flat card that appears more contemporary and current. One family used a 4" x 11" flat card to highlight, "What I loved about Grandma." Each of the children and grandchildren put in their special memory.
2. A traditional program that can include additional information and photos used as a takeaway or remembrance. These can be uniquely personal and provide comfort.

3. A smaller card referred to as a prayer card or holy card. A prayer card can include a favorite poem, verse, or prayer and a picture of a favorite saint or image that reflects the spirit of the individual.

Any of these options could include a special image of a hobby that overlays any text. Maybe a fishing pole, a special car, or favorite piece of artwork. Some families include the order of service because it's important to help guests follow along and understand who is doing the readings, bringing the gifts, and serving as pallbearers. For attendees who knew your loved one in a professional setting, it can be helpful to see the names of children and family members. In a more informal setting, a non-traditional or creative program serves the purpose of a keepsake and an acknowledgement that the event has taken place.

Memory Tables/Photos/ Slideshows
In addition to the information, you leave for your loved ones on your funeral plan, some families create a memory table of their loved one. That display can include a range of items like high school sports items, pictures of their family of origin, wedding photos, favorite books, or awards won at work.

Recently, a family used several tables to give away their loved one's ties! The memory table could include handwritten notes, scouting paraphernalia, small mementos. Tri-fold poster boards filled with photos have almost been replaced with digital photos. We all have a lot of photos. For my mother's slide show, we had 472 photos. That woman loved to have her picture taken. How to best show digital photos? Most churches and venues have some A/V equipment to showcase and display slideshows. Some church services will show them during a visitation or luncheon. Others will showcase them prior to the service in the sanctuary. If you're in an event space, the slideshow can be played the entire time, if you choose. You can pick their favorite music to put with the slideshow (being cognizant of any music use rights). While most funeral homes can do this, with today's technology, most people under the age of 40 know how to put these together. Keep in mind two things. First, make sure you know what format the A/V equipment takes as an input for the venue if you need to bring a physical device with the slideshow. Increasingly, more places take the inputs from the cloud. Second, this makes a very nice family memento for everyone to have copy or access to it, following the service. Plan ahead—we don't know what the best medium will be to showcase photos or video ten years from now. Storing photos in a cloud format will be solid, but you'll need to leave directions on where to find them in the cloud. Using albums or shared albums within your phone provider's platform is a good start.

Memorial Gifts

Memorial gifts usually mean where/what organization you'd like money donated to in your memory. Like everything surrounding funerals, there are countless choices. In fact, recently a person who was planning their mother's funeral expressed they wanted their guests to give a friend a hug in honor of their mother. Another new practice is people suggesting taking a friend to lunch and reminisce with your fond memories of their mutual loved one. Families might direct friends to give to your favorite organization in honor of their loved one. Families often choose the organization that is most aligned with their family member's illness or cause of death such as the American Cancer Society or American Heart Association. You may have had a favorite way to spend time or an organization that you've invested a lot of time in such as the Girl Scouts, pet adoption agencies, or Boys & Girls Clubs.

A memorial gift could be for the church or children's organizations or a non-profit hospice firm the family used that was invaluable in their final days. These are all meaningful ways to direct funds. When dealing with a loss, families can agonize over where to direct these funds. It's best to choose no more than three options for these directives. Leaving this information or talking about it with a family member ahead of time is helpful. With the advent of digital giving, it's important to include the correct address or URL on where to donate. It can be helpful to let the charity know in advance that you're directing memorial gifts to them. Be sure to provide them with your contact information so they can provide you with a list of donors you can use to acknowledge their gift.

Pallbearers
A pallbearer is one of several participants who help carry the casket at a funeral. Some traditions distinguish between the roles of pallbearers and casket bearer. It's a lovely designation to have pallbearers and honorary pallbearers. Pallbearers usually sit with their family members and are used ceremoniously, to finish rolling the casket from the church to the back of the hearse/coach. They might be used at the cemetery depending on the funeral logistics for a gathering meal or coming straight to the cemetery. The funeral directors can handle pallbearer tasks for the family. In the event there are not people to designate, or their preferred pallbearers are elderly, they could be designated honorary pallbearers in the program. Unlike in the past, now women can be pallbearers. It's moving to see all ages of friends and family be designated pallbearers at a funeral.

What are your thoughts on ...
Service location? Secular, sacred, or no service?

Who should lead the service?

Eulogy: Who would you like to deliver it?

Poems/Prayers/Scripture: Do you have favorites?

Music: What songs or hymns will be played or sung?

Flowers (list):

- Traditional burial flowers

- Memorial service flowers

- Gravesite flowers

Picture: Identify or attach your preferred photo for your loved ones.

Programs: Contemporary or traditional?

Memory tables/photos/slideshows: Where are pictures kept and how can they be identified?

Memorial gifts: Where to send contributions in your name?

Pallbearers: In person or honorary? Who?

Other Thoughts...

"What you leave behind is not what is engraved in stone monuments, but what is woven into the lives of others."

—Pericles

CHAPTER 3
What's It Going to Be?

Traditional Burial

A traditional burial typically means that the body is placed in a casket. The body may be embalmed or un-embalmed, depending on the wishes of the family. It may be present at a service and then taken to a cemetery for burial. At the cemetery, it may be placed in the ground or placed in a mausoleum. While traditions vary from culture to culture, this is what defines the funeral choice as traditional. Families pick traditional burials for several reasons. This could be a familial decision that comes with a great deal of comfort. Often people are comforted knowing that grandma was buried, mom was buried, and they could also be laid to rest with their family. That comfort also comes from personal history with religious rituals and experiences. Whether Catholic, Jewish, or another religion, a traditional burial has been the norm for the last several decades. There might even be a family plot with availability. That might make it an easier choice. By leaving the details of your traditional funeral choices with your family, it's a decision your family members can make with confidence.

When deciding on a traditional burial, there are several other costs to consider. Let's start with the burial itself—a local burial is straightforward. You may already own a plot, there may be a family plot. If not, this is something to proceed with now. Location, location, location. The piece of property will only get more expensive from now until you need it and then it may already be sold. The concept of cemetery property rarely includes a deeded piece of property that you own. It's typically a piece of property that you have the right to bury your loved one in. Those rights are managed by a cemetery association or corporation and differ from property to property. Even if a cemetery and funeral home are located together on the same property, with the same owner or corporation, they are typically two transactions. One for the traditional funeral decisions, casket, body preparation, cars, flowers, etc. The second transaction covers all things burial including cemetery plot, outer burial container, open and closing fees, and any ongoing maintenance fees.

Cemeteries

If you're selecting a traditional burial, identify where you want to be buried. What are the options for your hometown cemetery, veterans' cemetery, or your own backyard? This information is important to leave to your loved ones. A hometown cemetery is quite desirable; however, when making that choice, check and see how it's funded. Is there an endowment to secure long-term upkeep of the cemetery? We've all been to or seen overgrown, unmowed, or untrimmed cemeteries that look awful! You likely don't want such an environment for your final resting place. Sometimes smaller cemeteries are managed by the city or county. Other times, they might be owned by the church or Catholic diocese. If the cemetery is owned by a corporation or is privately managed, ask about the long-term funding plan for the cemetery.

The next question you need answered is about any requirements the cemetery has for a vault or outer burial container to hold the casket. Have you ever walked in an older cemetery and the ground is uneven, with your ankles moving unsteadily? Burial vaults were originally called "rough boxes." In the late 1700s, the need for more protection of the casket, unfortunately, arose through grave robbing. There was also a time in history when thieves stole bodies to sell to medical schools looking for cadavers for anatomical studies.

Most cemeteries did not require an outer burial container until the mid-20th century, but the earliest use can be traced to the 1700s. You may still find cemeteries that do not require this step.

Historically, wooden caskets broke down due to the elements as did the ground above the casket, resulting in uneven terrain. That's difficult to maintain from a landscaping perspective. In response, cemeteries began requiring some type of outer burial container to maintain lawn consistency. The industry identified an opportunity to upsell and cross-sell consumers, prompting the swell of vault companies. Even though the casket had been exposed to the elements in the ground including groundwater, now there was a dictated need to protect the casket from the elements. Consider the options of "good," "better," and "best" for outer burial containers and vaults that people purchase for their loved one's interment. This is not a funeral home requirement or state requirement; the need for an outer burial container is a requirement of the cemetery. Typically, an outer burial container is made of concrete and meets the basic cemetery requirements. Sometimes a cemetery will require a sealed vault. This offers additional water protection than concrete, but it will never be labeled waterproof by the company selling it. At the high end, there are outer burial containers made from bronze or stainless steel.

A mausoleum may be the choice of the family to lay their loved one to rest. It's a building that might be accessed from inside or outside and is constructed as a monument to enclose the deceased. They might be more common in places that are at risk of flooding. A mausoleum crypt inside a building might be appealing to visit your loved ones without worrying about the weather. There could be additional spaces together for a family or you could pursue a private mausoleum that's just for your family. Mausoleums are also called house niches for cremains and cremation urns.

A person can be buried on their own property if local ordinances are followed. Permissions may or may not be outlined by your HOA. If you are part of a rural community or on your own property, permission for burying a traditional casket or cremains would be outlined within the county structure.

Traditional Caskets

Have you ever met one person who's eager to go into a casket display room? Neither have I. Whether it is a display room with full caskets or the more current display room of ¼ caskets, it's difficult. In today's world of all things digital, a digital photo of a casket can provide a lot of confidence when making your selection.

We are going to go, what are we going in? There are basically three options for caskets—metal, wood, and biodegradable. To make it easier to start the conversation, does a family prefer wood or metal? Some people grew up in an area of forests and that's why they would select wood. Other families, mindful of costs, will select a metal casket. Those are typically slightly less expensive and come in a wide range of colors.

After the decision of wood or metal is made, there are multiple types of wood and grades of metal to consider. There are even some new casket choices made from barnwood. A veneer or poplar casket can help conserve costs. A mahogany casket is beautiful and offers a rich finish. I once helped a family that loved the finish on their casket for their son, who suffered an untimely death. That he was buried in essentially a beautifully made piece of furniture helped give them peace. There is not a right or wrong choice.

History of Caskets

In the United States, the early casket industry evolved from local furniture and cabinetmakers who doubled as undertakers. They built wood caskets on an as-needed basis. During the Civil War, thousands of coffins were needed to transport dead soldiers, marking the start of the mass-produced casket era. The casket industry traces its roots back to ancient Egypt and Mesopotamia, where wood, cloth, and paper were used to make stone sculpture-style burial boxes. In Europe, the Celts began making caskets out of flat stones around the year 700. However, for centuries, caskets were only used to bury aristocrats and nobility. Most bodies were simply wrapped in burial shrouds.

In the United States, casket manufacturing developed in the late 19th century. Steel caskets first appeared in the late 1840s, when Almond Fisk received a U.S. patent for a cast-iron casket that he claimed was airtight and indestructible. The bronze-finished "metallic burial case" featured a lid made from a sheet of glass, which allowed mourners to view the deceased. According to the Casket & Funeral Supply Association of America (CFSA), casket manufacturing developed as a separate business in the late 19th century. However, most companies only operated in local and regional markets.

By the early 1950s, the CFSA says there were more than seven hundred casket manufacturers in the United States. However, after decades of consolidation, only one hundred forty-seven companies were still active in 2003. Today, less than a dozen manufacturers assemble more than 90 percent of all metal caskets sold in the United States. CFSA estimates that three companies (Batesville, Aurora Casket Co., and York Group) produce more than 70 percent of all caskets sold annually. In 2023, casket manufacturing in the United States was a $668.3 million industry and experiencing declines of .2%-.5% every year.

Casket Options

There are so many choices. You can choose wooden caskets. You can choose handmade wood caskets. You can choose caskets made from bamboo or wicker. You can choose stainless steel, copper, or bronze caskets. Metal caskets are made in 18- to 20-gauge steel. They can be sealed or not have a gasket around the casket to seal. Cases can be made for or against those sealed/unsealed decisions. Metal caskets are lighter in weight. In a funeral home, only a small number of casket options may be on display. You should feel free to ask to see a printed or digital photo of their entire range of casket options. The interiors of caskets are usually not interchangeable. They're usually only available as shown in the photo—often tufted, delicate, simple.

The interior cap panel may be able to be changed out with a saying or other embroidery detail. A recent trend is casket companies obtaining the licensing rights for a favorite college or brand. Those images may be used on the inside or outside of a casket.

Costco, Amazon, and other online vendors are selling caskets, and the FTC has specific language in place that requires your local funeral home to accept a casket from another funeral home, retail outlet, or manufacturer without imposing additional handling fees. The Trappist monks craft caskets out of pine, oak, cherry, or walnut. There are websites that sell caskets at unbelievable prices. Those are usually made in China. Another manner of personalization includes a basic casket hand-painted by friends. The finished product can be extremely beautiful and reflect the personality of the deceased which can give the family some peace at this difficult time. This method can be challenging to accomplish when someone dies suddenly. Some families purchase their wood caskets ahead of time. They use them for bookcases, coffee tables, or just store them in their home. Without personalization, most casket companies can deliver in one to four days to your home or to a funeral home.

No matter what the material, all caskets serve the same purpose—to lay your loved one to rest. A funeral director that's doing their job will show you caskets in a variety of price ranges and colors and get your feedback. Families often think this is the last thing they can do for mom or dad, and they want to buy the nicest (most expensive) casket. If that's their motivation, it's ok. A funeral director's role is to help the family make the best decision for them. Some families lean toward caskets that align with the colors of their favorite sports team or ones that match the colors of their home décor.

Custom Caskets

In recent times, casket companies have specialized in personalization. I currently have a metal casket at my house painted with my husband's college logo, all ready for him. How I have it is a whole different story. It will be perfect for him when the time comes, hopefully no time soon. In addition to companies that license logos and create custom caskets, there are ways to decorate your own casket or build your own casket. We had a family order a bright red casket and then ask a friend to paint it. Not knowing what to expect, this gentleman showed up with the finest of paints to delicately paint narrow stripes down the casket like you might see on a high-end sports car. The family loved it. After losing a child, a family who knew their daughter loved stickers invited everyone attending the service to walk by the casket and place a sticker on it. There were hundreds of stickers placed on her casket.

Custom end caps and panels provide ways to personalize the casket and make the funeral home more money. It's best to make these decisions as simple as possible. If a casket comes with personalization as in a military casket choice or maybe something that has a religious detail, that's another way to personalize.

One family selected a wood casket because their son was a basketball prodigy. During another visitation the father said to their friends standing next to his son's casket, "Isn't this a beautiful casket?" Those moments reveal it's not about the price, the interior, or the extras. It's about what brings you and your family member peace.

A story featured in *The New York Times* highlighted a neuro-surgeon faced with a debilitating disease who decided to build his own casket. The juxtaposition of someone facing their own mortality and deciding to face that mortality and build his own casket takes this discussion out of isolation and into the light. With this gentleman's interest in woodworking, working alongside a woodworker was the way he processed his journey. He inscribed the casket with the phrase, "I've loved the stars too fondly to be fearful of the night."

Natural Caskets/Biodegradable/Shrouds

There are several options for a natural burial. If you're looking for a more peaceful burial with the body being laid or carried into the gravesite, then a natural or green cemetery is another option. While those terms have several interpretations, there are biodegradable caskets made from willow that are prepared to be placed in the ground just like a traditional casket.

Placing a willow casket in the ground achieves a completely biodegradable burial experience. However, a cemetery that has a requirement for outer burial containers or vaults would not accommodate the expectation of a natural burial.

A natural burial can be a personal preference or meet a religious requirement. Whether a Jewish or Muslim funeral, there are ritual guidelines that also require a natural casket or all wood casket so that it's touching the earth. Some cemeteries that require an outer burial container will assist in meeting these requirements. The outer burial container, whether it's made of concrete, a pre-fab medium, or stainless steel, helps level the ground at the cemetery for maintenance and supports the personal requirements. Does the thought of a casket give you claustrophobia? Another option is to be buried directly in the ground in a cloth covering or shroud.

Green Funeral

If ashes to ashes, dust to dust is your preference, then you might consider being buried in a biodegradable casket or burial shroud in a cemetery that doesn't require an outer burial container. This is known as a green funeral experience.

My firm received a call from a woman who wanted to come in and meet. She looked healthy but had a terminal illness. She was interested in being buried in a shroud and asked if we knew of a cemetery that could accommodate her wishes. We were aware of a piece of land in the middle of a busy county, where the property owners had wanted to make it available for a natural/green cemetery. There was still availability, which allowed the woman to purchase a plot of land. When she passed, we took her un-embalmed body to the cemetery. A few friends had gathered and four of us were able to lift her into the grave and lay her to rest wrapped in her shroud. Her face was then covered, and the friends helped fill the grave. It was a completely peaceful experience that happened exactly how she wanted it to occur.

What are your thoughts on ...
If you are making a traditional decision, what are your
thoughts around:

Cemeteries?

Casket choice?

Green funeral elements ?

"I am ready to meet my maker. Whether my maker is prepared for the great ordeal of meeting me is another matter."

—Winston Churchill

CHAPTER 4
Ashes Aren't Really Ashes

Cremation History

The definition of the word cremation is "the act of reducing a dead body to ashes by fire, especially as a funeral rite." The practice of cremation on open fires was introduced to the Western world by the Greeks as early as 1000 BCE. They seem to have adopted cremation from some northern people as an imperative of war, to ensure soldiers slain in alien territory a homeland funeral attended by family and fellow citizens. The word is first traced to being used in 1620–1630. In Christian countries, cremation fell out of favor. When the family receives the remains of their loved one, they are often referred to as the ashes. This isn't technically true. Instead, the remains are the bones that are then processed to become ashes.

There is a growth in cremation for several reasons. Some people feel that it gives you more freedom in how you honor someone's remains. With a transient society, this gives you the opportunity to keep your loved one with you at all times or to scatter them in a place that's important to your family. Costs are another reason for the advent of cremation. Many families do not have the financial resources for a traditional funeral. Cremation has gained acceptance as a less expensive and respectful choice. What happens if cremation is selected? The funeral home will pick up your loved one and the family will be asked if there's anyone that would like to see the body prior to cremation. If so, there are a couple of options.

The body will be held in a refrigerated unit until the family has signed the authorization for cremation, the doctor has signed the death certificate, and depending on the state, a county coroner may need to review the death certificate and offer their authorization to proceed with cremation. There could be a wish for a final viewing. If so, that can be handled and there may be an additional cost. After that, the funeral home proceeds with the cremation process.

Ashes

In the funeral industry, ashes are technically referred to as cremains. Many people bury the cremains. Like a casket, their loved one has a final resting place, marked by a grave marker, or maybe interred in a funeral mausoleum. The cremains can also be split to bury or spread to honor whatever the family chooses. Or perhaps there are three children, and each would like a portion of the cremains. You might be surprised by how few urns are sold for cremations at the time of someone passing. It could be that families are waiting for a second parent to pass so they can be buried together in one urn. Or maybe it's just too hard to deal with the finality of the loss and they're waiting.

There are times when people want the ashes mailed to other family members or even a cemetery. The ashes can be mailed through USPS. However, UPS and FedEx do not transport human cremains.

Cremains can be carried on a plane. To do so, ask your funeral provider to provide a burial transit permit. You give the permit to TSA to avoid any tampering with the ashes. Even if you are only transporting a portion of the cremains, that document will explain the contents of the bag or box.

Often cremains are part of a service in a church or other celebration of life. It's important in the Catholic church that ashes are blessed as part of the Mass of Christian Burial. Families frequently decide to have the cremains at a celebration of life. Others choose not to have the cremains as part of the service. This is a personal family decision. Your faith community might have direction for you if that aligns with your religious communities' guidelines.

Kinda Green

A cremation can also be considered a green funeral. The body is reduced to bones and then ashes that can be buried. If you're worried about taking up space in the world, the ashes can be placed in a jar and even stored in a closet. If your green measurement is based on carbon dioxide emissions, then cremation might not be considered an option. The typical cremation requires a retort (cremation chamber), a purpose-built furnace, but there are other cremation alternatives such as alkaline hydrolysis and terramation of human composting. One eco-friendly cremation alternative is alkaline hydrolysis. Some people think about this alternative as "one final soak." Alkaline hydrolysis is a process that uses water, potassium hydroxide, and heat to reduce the body down to nutrient-rich liquid and bone.

Unlike traditional flame cremation, alkaline hydrolysis uses far less resources and energy. It uses one-quarter the overall energy of flame-based cremation and does not release the same pollutants into the atmosphere. As an alternative to cremation, it is more earth friendly.

In fact, the greatest drain on resources for this method of disposition is water usage. Alkaline hydrolysis uses about 300 gallons of water per person undergoing the process. This is equivalent to the amount of water the average person will use over the course of three days. It seems like a lot, and it is! However, because this alternative is so eco-friendly that used water (called effluent) is high in nutrients and beneficial to the planet, it can safely go into local municipality's sewer systems or fertilize non-edible plant life. While it can go safely into sewer systems, it is up to each state, county, or city if they want that water to go into their sewer systems. This led to slow adoption of this technology.

The leading eco-friendly cremation alternative is terramation, also known as human composting and natural organic reduction. Terramation uses plant matter to help natural decomposition turn the body into soil. During the process, heavy metals are removed from the soil. Additionally, pathogens cannot survive the temperature inside the vessel. In this way, it is the best alternative to cremation.

Terramation's ecological footprint is small. Most of the energy used goes towards keeping the facility's lights on! Each vessel is monitored for temperature, oxygen flow, and moisture levels. That technology also uses very little energy.

The energy used during terramation is far less than that of cremation and even less than alkaline hydrolysis. Terramation does not require the heating or cooling of retorts or water. It just requires the organics (plant material) that surround the body and time. Sustainably grown and harvested organics fill each vessel. The planet can handle that!

The more people that go through the terramation process, the more accurately we understand its impact on society and the environment. As it stands now, terramation seems to use about 1/6 to 1/8 the energy used for cremation. On the other hand, cremation uses energy over a roughly three-hour period (for one cremation). That is a huge difference and makes an incredibly small eco-footprint for terramation. This is a very new technology and in the funeral industry change can be very slow to new adoption.

Some corporate-owned cemeteries are dividing part of their real estate for natural burials. In several parts of the country, cemeteries are committing to a complete natural burial experience. This translates in different ways: no headstones or markers, or even GPS coordinates. When visiting or laying your loved one to rest, you may not see anything that identifies your loved one's plot. Without identifying markers, it can be a beautiful and peaceful place. There are companies that make beautiful, embroidered shrouds for burial or your loved one can be placed in their favorite blanket. Any option considered must align with cemetery requirements.

Urns

Approximately 20 percent of ashes are buried or placed in a columbarium. They do not need an urn to be buried or placed. The traditional urn shape now has some competition from other vessels that can also hold ashes.

Cremains are usually returned to families in a heavy plastic sack that's placed in a black plastic box. Any vessel that has an opening of approximately 4" and is at least 6" x 6" x 6" can hold the ashes of an average size adult, about five lbs. You can find decorative vessels at TJ Maxx or Hobby Lobby or other home goods stores. Some families use a small suitcase to reflect someone's love of travel. Some use decorative ginger jars in their loved one's favorite color that can blend into the decor and no one would know they're holding your loved one's cremains. There are also keepsake urns that hold a small number of ashes to keep a little bit of your loved one close.

For those who wish for a green burial there are urns made from old railroad ties or fence posts and biodegradable urns made from salt or sand. Also, there are large biodegradable envelopes that can be used to float and sink in water or bury under a tree.

Scattering the Ashes
This is an idea that offers people a lot of peace, dust to dust. Before you spread ashes in a loved one's favorite place such as a golf course, lake, or ocean, you must check if there are regulations for placing or scattering ashes in a public place. For some, the love of these iconic landscapes appears to be the perfect location for the final resting place for their loved one.

Several national parks allow the practice, but always check park websites for information about permit requirements for scattering ashes which are regulated on a park-by-park basis. Generally, parks ask that you leave no markers and avoid environmentally sensitive areas. This can be as simple as selecting undeveloped areas away from the public portions of the parks. Unlike the majority of national parks, national forest lands do not allow scattering.

Cremains are made up of bone material and they don't automatically soak into the ground with water. Ask permission before scattering ashes on private property. If you choose a favorite city park or even a cemetery, you need to get permission to scatter. Don't attempt to secretly scatter ashes. That's trespassing. Sport stadiums, golf courses and amusement parks are private property. Your loved one's favorite sports team's end zone wouldn't be the place to secretly stash even a small amount of cremains. If caught, the police could be called which might result in a fine or community service. Then the ashes still need to be moved, if they are recovered. This likely isn't the scenario you anticipated to respect and honor your loved one.

Spreading ashes at sea is allowed, but any vessel or bag must decompose easily. According to the EPA, burial at sea of human remains—cremated or not—is permitted, but there are several scattering ashes laws and regulations that you need to follow.

- Any type of remains, including ashes, can only be placed in the ocean three nautical miles from land or more.
- Ashes can be scattered from a boat or airplane.
- Only biodegradable urns may be used. Anything placed in the water must easily decompose in a marine environment.
- You can release flowers or wreaths into the water, but they must decompose easily.
- While a permit is not required, you must report the burial to the EPA within 30 days.
- Pet cremains may not be spread at sea without a special permit.

Most rivers, ponds, and lakes are not subject to federal regulation, and therefore federal scattering ashes laws do not apply. However, it would defer to the cemetery board, environmental agencies, state, county, or city regulations, where you want to spread the cremains to learn more about the relevant laws. You need to contact the mortuary board, environmental agency, or health agency in the state where you want to spread the ashes to learn more about the relevant laws. Scattering ashes in inland waters is illegal in some states.

Many states also have laws related to spreading ashes that prohibit cremains from being scattered on beaches or shore-lines. Some states, such as California, do permit it as long as you're five hundred yards from shore. So many people have unique, different ideas for laying ashes to rest. It is important to research those options for what is allowed on a city/coun-ty/state and federal level.

There are firms that scatter ashes in professionally created, commercial grade fireworks. Most memorial fireworks use approximately three tablespoons of cremated remains loaded into a fireworks shell. There are firms across the country that can provide the display, or you can purchase the fireworks to launch yourself. There are companies with drones, gliders, and hot air balloons that transport the ashes all the way to the outer limits of the Earth's atmosphere and release them. You can hire a cruise ship to scatter them and even have them blown into glass.

How about storing ashes in a stuffed animal, jumping out of a plane, and scattering them on the way down, or burying them under a tree? Churches and city parks might have a scattering garden or a place to bury ashes. With no marker, perhaps a beautiful garden can bring peace.

How does the body leave the casket for the crematory? There are rental caskets that open the end and a sturdy cardboard container with the body can be removed and prepared for cre-mation. These costs are like a traditional burial, but it's a nice option for many families.

What are your thoughts on ...

If your choice is cremation, what are your thoughts regarding:

Cremation?

Viewing prior to cremation?

Urns?

Where to place the ashes?

Who will get ashes?

Will they be shared?

With whom?

"If I had a flower for every time I thought of you, I could walk in my own garden forever."

—Alfred Tennyson

CHAPTER 5
Elements

A funeral or memorial service reflects your cultural, spiritual, and religious beliefs. It also reflects the personality of the deceased and the loved ones who are planning the service. As such, every funeral is unique. However, some elements of a funeral are common to most memorial services and funerals.

Whether or not certain elements will be included and the order in which the elements are presented depends on personal preference. However, if you plan a funeral, the list can help you decide what elements to include. You are not limited to these components, and you are not required to include them all.

A funeral service has two primary functions: to acknowledge the death and lifetime achievements of an individual and to bring grieving family members and friends together in support of one another.

There are countless options for this memorable occasion. Loss affects everyone differently and how we choose to honor a loved one is as unique as the individual. For families everywhere, a funeral service can mean many different things. My family has always been a little untraditional. Even though all my grandparents were buried, my parents were focused on cremation, and they chose that for my sister who died in 1992. My maternal and paternal grandparents had a variety of traditional and graveside only services. Even within just one family, one marriage, there were options to consider. This is another reason it's so important to capture your wishes.

Service Structure Options
The objective of a visitation is to greet family members and convey condolences. This traditionally occurs the day before the funeral and usually takes place at a funeral home. Depending on the age of the deceased and the number of surviving family members, a traditional visitation can take around two hours or last several days.

Visitors have a few minutes to speak directly with family members to share sympathies and memories. Without exception, family members appreciate that someone took the time to come and pay their respects. Whether a few people show up or there are hundreds, it's a lovely memory for the family. We've had visitations when a young person has passed with a thousand people attending. No matter the duration, visitations can be completely overwhelming but deeply comforting to the family.

With new directions on funerals, there are new combinations for visitations and funerals:

One-Day Visitation/Funeral
The objective of a funeral service, no matter the duration, is to provide hope and closure, and pay tribute to your loved one. More and more in this busy life, we're seeing a one-day event with visitation and service and reception/lunch on the same day. It can be especially hard on young families to rally for two days of activities. Visitations can be shortened to an hour or two prior to the funeral service. Another option is for the family to show up for the service and then greet their guests at

a small reception after the service. In that case, a traditional burial can be postponed for several hours and then attended by family members and close friends. When the burial takes place immediately after the service, it can be difficult for older friends and family members to attend both functions and then return for the meal which is often held at the church. Be mindful that some cemeteries charge overtime after 2:30 p.m., so that's a consideration when planning.

Two-Day Visitation/Funeral

The two-day visitation/funeral has long been the practice for decades. The activities may start with a visitation at a church or funeral home the night before the service. If you have a big family or are expecting a large turnout, sometimes the two-day funeral works well. You can greet your friends the night before in a more formal receiving line. When holding a visitation the night before a funeral, about half of the attendees will go to the visitation, and the rest will attend the service the next day. Offering two opportunities helps to manage the number of people that your church or venue holds. For example, with a visitation the night before, you can expect half that number to attend the service the next day. The funeral can be followed by a reception after the service, offering an additional chance to visit with family and friends. With a traditional casket service, the burial can occur after the luncheon or reception and would probably just be attended by family and close friends. It's typical that some people will only attend certain parts of the overall funeral while others will attend all parts including the visitation, funeral, burial, and luncheon/reception.

Whether a one-day or two-day visitation/funeral, there are personal preferences for an open or closed casket. Some families relate to their religious or family ritual of having an open casket while other families are uncomfortable with a public viewing of their loved one.

Graveside-Only Service

This can be a very nice way to lay your loved one to rest. In its simplicity, people gather at the gravesite. Tent and chairs can be provided by the cemetery. On a good weather day, even with cold temperatures, being open to the sky can really make for a beautiful setting. Most cemeteries can provide a tent and chairs for six or twelve people. If perhaps just one person needs a chair, you can always bring a folding chair to the service for that individual.

A graveside service usually lasts around fifteen minutes, but there are elements like singing or playing an instrument that can add beauty and time to the service and setting. We often see bagpipers that are a distance away but add a lovely signature with a favorite song of the family or loved one. Often families have the graveside service first and can then proceed to a service or celebration of life. This can be the preferred method for several religious denominations, where the casket is not usually present at the church.

A service can be held later, for traditional burials or for cremation. The benefit of cremation is that there is no hurry. The cremation can take place and then a family gathering can be scheduled, maybe around a birthday or anniversary. That gives family more time to schedule for the committal service. A committal service is an organized time at a cemetery for a pastoral blessing or brief remarks. The committal service can be for traditional burial or for placing ashes in a columbarium, which could be located at a cemetery, church, or at a mausoleum. A traditional burial can be held from one to two weeks after passing, maybe longer in some specific circumstances.

With the awareness of all these options, it reinforces the importance of giving your loved ones direction on your wishes. Your family will appreciate knowing and be relieved that they have guidance to follow.

Permission

Sometimes people need permission to do something different. The service or gathering doesn't have to be like great grandma had for her funeral, starting with the location. Where would you like to have the service? Over 50 percent of weddings are no longer held in a church. Funerals are another occasion where folks consider alternative locations for a variety of reasons. The church that your parents grew up in might not be where they currently attend church. They might feel that their childhood church doesn't want them back, since they weren't regular attendees. I've never seen that situation. Many denominations welcome helping a family during this time, and they want to be the church that cares for grieving people. As a good pastor friend of mine said once, "If your children only came home on Easter and Christmas, would you be excited to see them?" I believe the church feels the same in caring for the brokenhearted.

Consider what details best illustrate a life well-lived and honors our loved one. One of the first questions is where to have the service. Nothing is off the table. From a picnic shelter at the local park for a young mom to the biggest cathedral in the city for a civic or business leader. A celebration could be held in your home church, your backyard, or favorite coffee shop.

It might be in a funeral home. The setting could be formal or casual. The gathering can be private or live streamed. It could be held in a sports stadium. Here's an interesting perspective. Our company's accountant was a complete outdoorsman. One of his adventurous pursuits was hiking the Pacific Crest Trail. His family wanted his funeral outdoors and held it in a natural amphitheater at our local arboretum.

The important thing is that it works for you and the people who might attend. We never know for certain how many people will attend but make sure to use a space that can accommodate the number of at least your anticipated guests. Your funeral home professionals can assist in this, but you know your family best.

In recent times, some people are saying they don't want a service. That may be your choice. If so, that's important to communicate to your loved ones.

Home Funerals
This is a concept that has several different interpretations and can be manifested in different ways. Whether it's honoring your loved one based on a religious ritual in your home for the first twenty-four hours after death or a true home funeral, you may need guidance from your state or county.

A home funeral is a time-honored way of families caring for their own loved ones after death. It provides families with a slowed down, carefully planned for, more affordable, hands-on experience.

It's not a new concept. Not long ago, families were completely responsible for the preparation and burial of loved ones' bodies after death—it was considered an ancient art, an honor, an act of respect and compassion and a very natural part of the grieving process.

In the past, loved ones were laid out at home in the front room or parlor and neighbors, family members, and friends all gathered together to care for their own, offering practical help and community support.

Today more and more families are reclaiming this right to hold a family-led home funeral. This involves family and/or friends gently washing and dressing a loved one's body which may include:

- Lovingly laying out the body at home
- Naturally cooling the body
- Bringing the body home (if death happens elsewhere)
- Gathering to share, grieve, and spend precious time

Funerals may be held at home, at any time and/or in any place of personal connection such as a church, temple, mosque, village hall, community center, sports club, and/or local hotel.

The significant difference with a home funeral is that you can stay in control of the process. You can choose where and when you hold the funeral and create a very personal ceremony which honors the life of your loved one.

You'll also choose whether your loved one's body will be buried or cremated and can arrange this to be unhurried and in accordance with their beliefs, values, and/or wishes.

The benefits of a home funeral can be many tender moments, loving care, knowing hands, more time to say goodbye. The true value of a home funeral lies in the extra time you spend tenderly caring for your loved one. Slowing down the process allows all involved to accept and absorb the death at your own pace. Home funerals are a gentle and loving way to keep everyone involved and families connected. They are more intimate, more meaningful, and ultimately allow for greater closure and healing.

Home funeral care can be a profound last act of love for a loved one. You have time to keep vigil, to sit and just be with the person, to grieve in your own home, with more time to say goodbye.

Burial Out of State

We are a transient people. Where we pass might not be the place that we are laid to rest. Maybe you're in one state with family for care, but your spouse or family members are in another state. You might have a family plot with space available and that's the best fit for your final resting place. Maybe there's no one in your immediate family that will be buried in your current state, so it doesn't make sense for you to be laid to rest all by yourself. Whether it's cremation or traditional burial, there are some things you need to know before you schedule and travel with your loved one.

If you choose to be buried with services in another state, you can be transported, typically by air, to a funeral home in that state. The body will be embalmed in the state where you passed and depending on the situation, the casket can be selected in that state or at the funeral home that you're being transported to. If the service will take place in the state where you passed, the casket can be transported to the state of your final resting place. However, you'll need to engage with a funeral home there to pick up the casket upon arrival and hold it until the graveside service occurs. All the details previously covered are still relevant, but they just might occur in two different states.

When arranging for a body to be sent to another state for burial or arranging for a body to be brought to your state for burial, there are several additional steps to consider. A body can be driven or flown to their final resting place. Typically, there are two funeral homes involved. One is responsible for the sending, and one is responsible for the receiving. The sending funeral home secures the flight and prepares the body for transport. The transfer may or may not include a casket but does involve an air tray. The receiving funeral home is responsible for picking up the body from the airport or receiving the body at the funeral home and then taking the next steps for service or burial. Bodies are flown on commercial airlines and aren't unloaded, instead they're taken to a different terminal or pickup for transport. Airlines practice discretion, which is why we don't see more air trays, the vehicle that bodies are placed into for transport when the luggage is being unloaded. At least I haven't seen any as a passenger. Flight costs for transporting bodies are consistent. They don't change based on promotions or passenger availability.

A licensed funeral home is necessary to pick up the body. There are certain numbers/bill of ladings required to make sure everything has been accomplished and paid for.

When a death occurs in a foreign country or someone needs to be sent to another country for burial, there are several

additional steps. It's important to select a firm with experience shipping a body overseas. Usually, bodies are cleared through certain custom hubs, before departing the country. If the paperwork isn't correct, the body will be sent back to the point of departure. It's also important to call multiple funeral homes to see how much they charge for this service. The price can vary by $10,000 or more, for the exact same service. If the death occurs overseas, the country's consulate can provide advice and assistance with the process. With the increased travel there is a specific insurance policy that will cover body transport at a reasonable price. Whether your wish is for cremation or traditional burial, that policy would go a long way to providing peace of mind as some countries take six weeks for cremation.

What are your thoughts on ...

Service location?

One-day visitation/funeral?

Two-day visitation/funeral?

Graveside-only service?

Home funerals?

"To the world you may be one person; but to one person you may be the world."

—Dr. Seuss

CHAPTER 6
Details, Details

Viewing

The core difference between visitation and viewing is how the deceased person's body is presented. With a viewing, the body is on display in a casket; a visitation can occur with a closed casket or without the body present. In the traditional structure of a two-day funeral service, the viewing could occur the day before the religious or memorial service. It might occur at the funeral home, or it could occur at the church. Most churches, not all, request that the casket be closed for the mass or service. The viewing, whether the day before or the day of the service, provides family and friends one last opportunity to see their loved one. Personal feelings about this practice vary. While some people don't like seeing their person "dead," they can also look more peaceful in repose than they did in their last days or weeks of suffering from their illness. A viewing can provide peace. Truly every decision should move you to one of peace. What brings you peace? What is your wish for your loved one and their peace?

A viewing prior to cremation can take place at a funeral home. Embalming does not need to take place for that to occur. The funeral home will have taken some steps for you or your loved one to look as if you're sleeping. Eyes and mouth will be closed. Covered with a blanket, head on a pillow. This can be important with sudden death or if your loved one lived out of town and they'd like to see you one more time.

If you've chosen traditional burial, with a service, viewing or visitation in an indoor location, then you may choose to have another time to spend with your family member. This could be a private family viewing time, or it could be open to the entire service. For a private or public viewing, it's important to select clothing that has long sleeves. For women, a round or higher neck blouse or jacket. Maybe a scarf that will add color around the face. Shoes are not necessary, but I personally would like to be buried in my UGG slippers. Socks are also not necessary, but whatever the family member wants to include is fine.

If someone wants to see their family member, every funeral home has different procedures to make sure that occurs. There may or may not be fees to view. These fees are tied to extra costs that are incurred by the funeral home. It may be related to transportation, cosmetology and/or the funeral home's procedures or state regulations on embalming. They'll make every effort to accommodate your family. What's even better? Ask your family that question prior to someone passing, even before someone is sick. Use *Before You Go* to develop your plan. Then, go to your family members and ask them their preferences about viewing others when the time comes. It can be a difficult question but better to address it now, well in advance.

Maybe someone wants to see their family member and even have them at the church for a traditional funeral, followed by a cremation. That's a common practice. This presents a way to combine preferences to get the best of both worlds, allowing the family to follow traditional rituals prior to cremation.

The ritual of lying in state works for traditional or cremation choices. It can happen for several hours or several days. It's set up in a room or private space at the funeral home or the church might provide an accessible space. People can come and sign the register book and pay their respects. The family doesn't have to be present for that acknowledgment, but depending on the length, the family could have one or two people present to greet their guests. This is much closer to a centuries-old experience of having a family member laid out in the parlor of the family home. That's rarely done today, but if it's appealing to you or your family member, it can be accomplished.

Something that can bring quite a bit of comfort is to include notes, photos, special memory items with your loved one, whether for cremation or traditional burial. In the case of a sudden death, those can be added to the cremation container, prior to cremation. Sometimes, families want to include a flower. These are important items because they bring peace.

Obituary

No way around it, the thought and process of writing an obituary for your loved one is hard. If you wait to write an obituary after your loved one has died, it could take a couple of days to write, review, and share it with other family members for their review. It's best practice to give others time to rewrite what you've written. Once complete, review it with fresh eyes one more time. The funeral director will advise on submitting it to your local paper, their publishing timelines and costs. It is widely known that big city newspapers charge exorbitant fees. One of the most helpful things you can do for your family is to write your own obituary ahead of time. If you at least draft your obituary and identify what's important to highlight or what to skip over, that gives your family a sense of what you deem meaningful. Is the chapter name of a group that you were a member of important? Does anyone in your family know what that is? Probably not. Helping them in their time of grief by preparing in advance for your passing will be a comfort when the time comes.

Develop the obituary in four sections.

1. The first section includes the facts of your life: date of birth, date of death, where you were born and your parents.
2. The second section includes the details of your life. This is where you list your schools, the name of your spouse or partner, names of children and other important family members, your professional and personal highlights. This is a time to highlight what your personal accomplishments were and what was important to you. What was fun and meaningful.
3. The third section notes those who have predeceased you and those who survive you.
4. The final section outlines the service details and where you'd like to direct any memorial donations in your name.

With the increasing cost of newspaper obituaries, many funeral homes are posting the full obituary on their own website, which should be of no charge to the family. In a newspaper obituary, you can include a photo and shortened obituary with a link that directs people to the funeral home website for additional details which saves money. The newspaper obituary might read something like "for a full tribute, please see www.funeralhome.com." A photo helps get attention in a larger newspaper but will increase your cost. A shortened obituary with a link is a way to manage costs and still leave a full remembrance for your loved one.

Also consider in which newspaper(s) you want the obituary published. Some choose their hometown as well as having it in the city newspaper where they live.

Social Media

Social media is a continually changing environment that everyone is learning to navigate. Leaving information about passwords and social media accounts is helpful for closing or leaving those accounts in a "memorial" status. Facebook and Instagram can designate a legacy contact. This is a task that can be done in advance and will allow posts and updates to be done by someone else when you pass. This is especially helpful when a death is unexpected. For some, this memorialization is a way to heal, while for others it can be a source of pain and a constant reminder of the loss. It's hard to tell how you're going to feel about it until you see the memorialized profile, so there's no need to be hasty in your decision. Give yourself time to figure out how you want this handled. Ultimately, it's up to you and your family how you want to deal with your loved one's digital legacy, taking into consideration what you think they would have wanted.

X doesn't offer any kind of memorialization; you can either keep their X account up or delete it. If you choose the latter, you'll need to contact X and submit a form with their name and X handle, as well as a copy of the death certificate. You'll also have to identify yourself and your relationship to the person. If further steps need to be taken on your part, X will email you to let you know what you need to do next. LinkedIn is an effective tool for sharing an obituary and service details if the deceased individual is employed or professionally active. This is often the only way to learn about the death of a colleague or professional acquaintance, if not connected to them in a personal social media forum.

With the cost of obituaries, especially in a larger city newspaper, social media can be the best way to communicate that someone has passed and provide the service details. A funeral home will place the obituary on its website, typically without a charge or word-count limitation. That link can be embedded in any social media, personal emails, or texts.

Funding
There are many items to be mindful of when considering expenses because they all add up. That's why I advocate for personal education about funerals and the options and choices available. Pre-planning and communicating those plans to family or friends as well as preparing a written document will leave no questions about your wishes. However, I am not a believer in pre-paying the funeral home for your funeral. However, there are situations that require people to pre-pay. For example, if you're trying to qualify for a Medicaid spend-down. In that case funeral expenses can be pre-paid and aren't counted against the total resources to qualify for Medicaid. If that isn't your situation, your money will grow quicker in your financial products than your funeral choices being "price protected" in a funeral trust. Different funeral homes offer different choices for pre-payment options. It might be an insurance policy. It might be a trust. It could be owned by the funeral home, or it could be managed by a bank. Different states have different regulations for managing this fund. Either way, you'll have the confidence that you have researched

and have placed the money in a designated account. Most funeral homes require payment twenty-four to forty-eight hours before the services. They might require payment prior to cremation. They might charge a fee for you to collect from your insurance policy. They might require more if you pay by credit card. So, by educating yourself on the costs and placing the money in your own financial product, you can keep track of the funds and know that they are dedicated to this expense.

There is one area where it may be wise to pay in advance—cemetery expenses. Buy the plot, pay the open and close, buy the outer burial container or the vault, and the marker. Whatever the cemetery offers for advance purchase, do so. If you wait until a cemetery space or plot is needed, it may no longer be available. Best to plan ahead and as always, let your family know your arrangements.

When budgeting for funeral expenses, these are some of the most important matters to consider. Think about your personal preferences and add items to your budget if necessary. Any remaining balance after funeral expenses are covered will be part of your estate.

- Funeral type: traditional or cremation; casket or urn
- Flowers
- Obituary
- Service honorariums
- Celebration
- Food and beverage: family meal before the ceremony, repass/repast meal
- Travel expenses: something to consider if family members such as grandchildren need assistance

Service Honorariums

Beyond the funeral home staff, there are so many people involved in funerals that work behind the scenes. The funeral home pricing should be listed on their website or easily accessible when you're in the funeral home. If you're working with a church or asking someone to lead the service or play music or broadcast the service, it's important to offer a monetary gift for their assistance. Some churches have a printed list of honoraria fees that they give to the family, to set the appropriate expectation. Others say, "Oh whatever you would like to give." Sometimes the church itself has a fee and they distribute the honorariums to the AV/video resource, to the altar servers, to the organists, to the singer. The pastor or priest usually receives a monetary gift as well. If the family wishes to host a lunch at the church, some churches may cover that through their budget for ministry, but a lot of churches may not have that in their budget and charge a fee. They may not have the resources to prepare and serve the food as was typically done in years past, and instead, use outside catering. It is customary and a kind gesture to make an offer to anyone who is assisting with the service. If it's a friend, they may not accept it, but it's best to offer. Anyone assisting with the service is spending at least two hours on the day of the service and probably other time in rehearsals or preparation for the service.

Live Streaming

Technology. We can't live with it, and we can't live... well, we can't live without it. With the introduction of several different types of streaming platforms, there are several ways to open your funeral service to out-of-town or ill attendees. If you do so, keep several things in mind. You may not want it opened beyond the in-person guests. A live stream video includes the possibility that it will be out for perpetuity. COVID prompted many churches to get their electronic infrastructure up to speed. It's now common to use that to provide a video feed for funerals. Whether they provide it over a Facebook feed, or over their own network, it's a lovely way to communicate and capture the day.

A funeral is a time for hope and memories. The words, messages, people, and tributes can continue to bring peace to your family and loved ones, after the service. On that day, they may be full of grief and overwhelmed with activities, friends, and support, and revisiting the funeral stream soon after or even years later, can help bring peace. Your church or venue may have a proprietary platform for providing the link, so it's up to them how long the video is available post service. Facebook is a very reliable platform for live streaming, but now they have control and influence over the link. A funeral is such an emotional time that it's truly hard to remember what memories were shared or words that brought you comfort. A live stream that can be saved is a wonderful way to capture those memories, capturing people at a certain time or age, of a family as they gather. Sometimes, I hear well, this is a strange time to take photos or family pictures but since large family gatherings can be so infrequent, you should consider doing so. Just be sure to discuss it and get input from others.

It's easy for a friend or family member to hold up an iPad or phone for their own Facebook stream and post or email it later. Your funeral home might provide this service or help you find a professional video source to assist. Some higher-end video firms may have packages that take the video and merge it into a film with photos and special mementos to highlight the life of your loved one.

Some churches automatically provide a live stream. If you'd rather that not occur, communicate this with your family.

Family Cars/Coach/Hearse
First, the casket needs to get wherever it's going. Is it going to the church or to the gravesite? Is it family only? Do you even need a coach/hearse? A coach is what they call it in the funeral business. A coach parked outside a church, or any funeral service gives everyone a heads up that there's a traditional casket inside. It's a sign of respect to have the deceased be transported in a coach/hearse. If the casket is at the gravesite ahead of anyone being there, then bringing the casket to the church or gravesite in a minivan (the usual transportation vehicle for anything outside of a funeral) can save money. If there is a visitation or service and everyone is going to see the casket placed into a car, it does NOT LOOK GOOD to be placed into a minivan. It is and looks more respectful, in that situation, to be placed into a coach. Coaches are usually priced for a four-hour period, then charged for every additional hour. Using it just for a departure could be the same price as having it present for the entire service.

Family cars are a lovely option when you have multiple stops in the day. It's also extremely helpful if there's family in from out of town and they're not sure where they're going. A family car can start at one house, take you to the service, take you to the gravesite, and then back to the starting point. Or they can start at the church, take you to the gravesite and then back to the church. On a day that's filled with moving parts, it can be nice not to remember where your keys are and let someone else handle the driving. The funeral home can arrange for family cars.

House Sitting

Having an obituary published in a newspaper or on a funeral home website can, sadly, alert criminals that your home may be unattended during funeral activities. I think it's important to have someone watch over the house for you when the events are being held. Preferably, someone would stay at the house during the visitation, service, burial, and luncheon or reception. At the minimum, you could ask a neighbor to watch over the house.

What are your thoughts on ...
A viewing?

Obituary: Feel free to write it and leave it for your loved ones.

Social media: Would you like it announced before the service with the service details or after the service? Have you identified legacy contacts for someone else to access and update your account?

Funding: Do you want to include money for the service and service honorariums, for a celebration, for travel for family members? Where is the money kept and who can access it? Do you have a budget that you would want someone to adhere to?

Live streaming?

Would you like to use family cars for travel to the service and/or graveside?

House sitting?

> ## "*Life has to end. Love doesn't.*"
> —Mitch Albom

CHAPTER 7
It's My Party, I'll Cry If I Want to

Celebrations

Irish wakes, often simply referred to as a wake, are a celebration of life—one last party to honor the deceased. The term "wake" originated because unknown diseases had plagued the Irish countryside causing some to appear dead. As the family began to mourn, the deceased would awaken. For this reason, the body is kept in the deceased's home for at least one night. Depending on your community and religious customs, the wake is still a relevant term. Some might consider this for the first night of the funeral service. This event might also include a viewing.

As with any significant occasion or milestone, meals and receptions are important elements of a funeral. When someone dies, the family often hosts a repass or repast meal. This is usually less formal than an actual funeral service or memorial and it's common for anyone who attends to join the gathering. Funeral meals have long been a tradition to honor the deceased with one last gathering before sending them off into their eternal rest. You might have heard this event called by many names, such as reception or wake. It doesn't matter what you call it, they all serve the same purpose: bringing family and friends together for an intimate remembrance of someone who was cherished in life. Whether they're open or private, these gatherings serve as an important time for friends and family alike to share their condolences with the bereaved while also celebrating the life of your lost friend.

The time following a service can serve multiple purposes and can help you heal. They serve to celebrate the life of your loved one and get support from family who want to stand by you through it all. The act should be celebrated to commemorate their life's work and stop dwelling on how they will never come back again for good times—it's time now for new memories!

Formal or Informal

What to do and what's best for your family? What would you like to happen? A potluck? A church reception? A country club gathering? A gathering at a favorite bar or park? What about an art gallery? So many things to consider to best represent the spirit of your family. Does your family have individuals that want to coordinate, plan, and cook? If not, this is not the time to try and coordinate an event. Funeral receptions and memorial services occur in a variety of settings from event spaces to community centers, where they have tables/chairs/AV equipment, and space for everyone. This allows families to use catering or bring anything from simple cookies and drinks to dinner and drinks. Many funeral homes are expanding their offerings to include catered meals following the funeral home service, providing one-stop shopping. Those receptions typically would not involve alcohol.

Locations

Do you belong to a tennis club or country club? Even if you're not a member, they're often looking for additional daytime business and are open to hosting non-members though you might need to be sponsored by a member. The typical church lunch following the burial is changing too. Often, families will gather for the luncheon immediately following the service. This prevents losing people who attend the service but don't have time to go to the graveside service and then return for the lunch. Having the lunch immediately after the service gives you more time to visit with your friends. If you decide to hold the meal prior to the graveside ceremony, just be certain to carefully schedule so you avoid potential overtime costs at the cemetery.

There's a variety of other locations to consider. What about hosting a golf tournament? How about having family members gather on your birthday to reminisce and celebrate? Maybe it's a picnic or a day at an amusement park? Here's a great example of personalizing a gathering. I had an acquaintance who owned a landscaping company. She had a family member who was in a car accident. She called me to talk through options if their loved one passed. She asked, "Could I have the service or gathering in my greenhouse?" Absolutely! "Could I serve martinis, my family member's favorite drink?" Absolutely! The more the celebration reflects you or your loved one's spirit through art, music, location, or joie de vivre, the better.

Celebrating Ahead
What about planning and holding your funeral ahead of time? That's right, you'd be attending your own funeral/party/celebration of you! A new trend is emerging, the rise of personalized and meaningful end-of-life celebrations with the person you're honoring in attendance.

How many times have you been at a funeral and been acutely aware that the person you're honoring would've loved the funeral? Maybe some of the components change but by being there and celebrating ahead, you or your loved one are present to share in and enjoy all the love and admiration.

These celebrations are as unique as the individuals they honor, reflecting their passions, personality, and legacy. From intimate gatherings in nature to lively parties filled with laughter and music, end-of-life celebrations are becoming more diverse and creative than ever before. When someone understands that they are in declining health, they can look at this event to be with others. If that proves too challenging, we're seeing videos that loved ones have made and have them shown at the service. This can happen in formal or informal settings. By celebrating a life well-lived, we not only honor the deceased but also find comfort and healing in coming together to reminisce and cherish them.

Gifts/Keepsakes

As we continue planning, you can see how it's possible to weave a meaningful thread with music, stories, scripture, and art. Think about additional ways to make it meaningful and paint a picture of your life. Were you a gardener? What about distributing a seed packet or a bag with a daffodil bulb? What about a favorite recipe on a recipe card or bookmark or even a book of favorite recipes? Favorite music? What about a playlist? Are you famous for loving chocolate? What about a favorite chocolate truffle or monogrammed piece of chocolate? I recently helped a family celebrate a woman who passed and she loved butterflies. Yellow was a common theme with the program and flowers. There were butterfly poems and even a knit butterfly that a friend made for the family and attendees. They painted a picture of their loved one and remembered her in a loving warm light.

What are your thoughts on ...

Celebrations Formal, Informal

Location of Celebration

Budget for Celebration including potential Family Dinners.
Where is the money located?

Keepsake Ideas for Funeral

"*Those who love deeply never grow old; they may die of old age, but they die young.*"
—Sir Arthur Wing Pinero

CHAPTER 8
Location, Location, Location

You have 5 minutes. If your loved one dies at home and isn't under hospice care, the first call you need to make is to the police. The police will come with your community's EMT, and they'll begin their investigation. If your loved one has been in poor health, the police will call their doctor to determine if they are agreeable to sign the death certificate.

The conversation could go like this, "Dr. Smith, I'm here with Mrs. Jones, she didn't wake up this morning. Her niece says she has been under your care. Are you willing to sign the death certificate for her?" The doctor may reply, "I haven't seen her in my care for 2 years. I'm not willing to sign the death certificate." If that's the case, the next step is to contact a county coroner to continue the investigation. That will delay the need to select a funeral home for several days.

If the doctor agrees to sign the death certificate, then the next question is, "Which funeral home do you want to call?" Yes, that's right. In this moment of confusion, grief, and shock, the police are waiting for your answer. There's no time for research or to price shop. To compare services and then decide on cremation or burial. With your mind whirling, who are you going to call? Your thought is probably to call the funeral home that you've driven by for the last thirty years. You know, the one on the corner, what's their name again?

This is why it's important to think about this ahead of the need. With just a little time and some research you can have the rough plan outlined. For instance, if you're interested in using a local firm, be sure to identify them. Some families look and select a firm because they want to do business with a local firm. Sometimes it might be important to select woman-owned firm or minority-owned firm. But if you wait to select a funeral home at the time of need, there isn't enough time, energy, or bandwidth to make those decisions. When in your life do you spend between $2,000 and $20,000 on an expense without doing research? That's exactly what happens every day when people are making funeral decisions.

Determine what's important to you. Working with a local firm or a corporate firm? It's hard to tell which firms are locally owned and which are owned by corporations. When a large corporation comes in to purchase a local firm, they sometimes keep the name of the local firm, and the ownership is unclear.

Many local firms are owned by large out-of-town corporations. For instance, in the Kansas City metro area there are very few locally owned funeral homes. You typically only make funeral home decisions two to four times in your life. It's a lot easier to recall the name of the firm that you've driven by for thirty years, than to take the time to research a funeral home. A family might think, "We loved using the Smith Funeral Home for grandmother and grandad. Of course, we're going to use them for mom and dad or we went to school with the Millers, the Millers were on the city council. Let's use the Miller Funeral Home. But then you remember. Oh yeah. The "Millers" sold the business years ago. They no longer live in this community. They have no control over pricing or corporate policies. Are they still the best funeral home for your family? Without prior research, there's no way to know. There may be a new player in the market that's a better fit for your needs.

After you've called the funeral home that comes to mind, transportation is arranged. You can change your funeral home decision. However, you'll need to pay a second transport fee to the second funeral home.

Selecting a Funeral Home

When selecting a funeral home, besides having insight into your decision for cremation or traditional burial, there are other things to consider.

- Do you want a traditional funeral in a church? Do you have a church home?
- Do you want the funeral in a funeral home chapel, in a park, or in another location?
- Do you want to have a service?
- Would it be better for your family to gather later for a celebration? Maybe around a birthday or anniversary, a family golf tournament or picnic?

All those decisions can make sure you're selecting a funeral home that's best aligned with your wishes. There's no need paying a large corporate funeral home with a large chapel, if your wish is to have a direct cremation with a service later.

These first steps are important as a foundation for the rest of the journey. Leaving the information clearly communicated to a spouse or all the children helps the next decisions come together more easily. It helps lay out possible service timelines, travel details, and communication to family and friends.

Funeral Homes: Does It Matter?

We don't want to think about our loved ones leaving us. It's too hard. It's too sad. It won't happen anytime soon. Will it ever happen? The fact is, not even one of us is getting out of this world alive.

It's going to happen and hopefully it will happen in the right order. Grandparents, parents, children, grandchildren. It's a little easier to take when it occurs in that chronological order. Understanding the process before someone gets sick eases the already difficult situation. It could be as simple as looking on-line at your city's different funeral homes and maybe making an appointment to visit. It may include discerning if they are a locally owned firm or a corporate-owned firm. Think about what matters.

It can be helpful to pick a funeral home that is geographically close to you. However, a good funeral home will offer to come to your home to meet. Maybe mom has passed, and you can't leave dad alone. Whatever the reason, don't hesitate to ask if they can come to your home. The funeral home can assist by coming to your home to pick up clothes and personal items. If you'd like to use a less expensive funeral that's a little farther away from your home, that might be worth a little bit longer drive.

The issue of transparency in the funeral industry is one that is just starting to take hold. Whether it's pricing, types of services, casket and urn availability, or even the terms that that funeral home uses, there are a number of ways to make sure you go into the funeral home meeting with educated, quality questions and information. With a plethora of online information, there is an abundance of details that you can research ahead of need, to make the best decision. By understanding what you are looking for in a service, you can approach that funeral home with educated questions and knowledge to get clear answers on what you'd like to occur.

Some things to consider: Does the funeral home post prices on its website? Does it have packages available and what do they include? How does it offer and sell caskets? What is a direct cremation and what are the steps for that process? Does it offer pre-paid funeral plans? Is that information held in a trust or as a life insurance policy? What are the costs associated with those plans? Do you need payment at the time of service, forty-eight hours before the service, or do you have payment plans? After putting together your funeral plan, you can go into these phone calls, website research, or meetings to get definitive answers to your questions.

What are your thoughts on ...
What is the funeral home that you would like the family to use? Contacts at the funeral home:

"Death is nature's way of saying, 'Your table is ready.'"
—Robin Williams

CHAPTER 9
Checklists

There is paperwork that has to be completed. It might be able to be completed online. But there are several authorizations and some details that need to be answered by the deceased family member's next of kin. These are important steps so make sure that you understand and don't hesitate to ask questions.

Death Certificate Information
Each state requires information to file a death certificate online. In most states, the funeral home initiates this process and it serves as official notification to the state and the Social Security Administration that a death has occurred. Following is information that might be required by your state. Usually, the hardest things to come up with are the Social Security number and mother's maiden name for the deceased individual. Having all this information ready will facilitate the process. It's also helpful to know that this information is necessary should you be conducting genealogical research. You can check your state's health department website to review their specific requirements for death certificates.

There is a slightly different process for cremation. A cremation authorization must be signed by the surviving spouse or the children. While it only requires one child to sign, it's best to make sure everyone is on board with the decision for cremation. Documenting your wishes will advance funeral planning. In some states and counties, the signature of the county coroner is required to authorize a cremation. This is also handled electronically. After the signatures are obtained, cremation can occur.

With a traditional burial, the death certificates can be issued prior to burial. These are usually sent out by the state or county registration/health department office. The length of time can vary from three days to more than four weeks depending on the state.

I would consider the below items as, the primary information that's needed.

Death Certificate Information includes:
1. Decedent name (first, middle, last)
2. Gender
3. Maiden name prior to marriage (if applicable)
4. Date of death
5. Age
6. Social Security number
7. County of Death
   a. Place of death (facility name, if applicable)
   b. Facility address, including city and state
8. Date of Birth
   a. Place of Birth
9. Did deceased ever serve in the Armed Services
10. Marital status
11. Surviving spouse, if applicable
12. Decedent mailing address (street, number, city, state, ZIP)
13. Inside city limits (yes or no)
14. Father's name (first, middle, last)
15. Mother's maiden name, prior to first marriage (first, middle, last)

16. Informant's name (first, middle, last)
    a. Informant's mailing address and phone number
    b. Relationship to decedent
17. Number of death certificates
18. Method of disposition (burial, cremation, donation entombment, other)
19. Name and location of cemetery if burial (city and state)
20. Decedent ancestry or ethnic origin: Italian, German, Dominican, Vietnamese, Hmong, French Canadian, etc. Hispanic Origin (yes or no). If yes, specify origin
21. Decedent race
22. Highest level of education completed at the time of death
23. Decedent's usual occupation (work done during most of working life. Do not use "retired")
24. Type of business or industry (do not give name of company)

Cremation Authorizations and Additional Forms

Each state will have different guidelines to meet for authorizing a cremation. Some states and counties include a review by their county coroner before a cremation can take place. Some funeral homes have policies and processes requiring a family member to identify their loved one, prior to a cremation. There might be additional forms to fill out as in embalming authorization and jewelry or personal item forms. There might need to be a healthcare acknowledgment of pacemakers or other medical devices that are present in the body, to create an awareness for the personnel conducting the cremation.

Family and Friends

Who would you want notified in case of an unfortunate situation such as death? Not many of us have physical address books anymore. Instead, notifications are now typically done through Facebook, LinkedIn, and other social media platforms. You may have strong opinions about using social media to communicate a death announcement so make sure your family is aware of your wishes. To further help your family, consider leaving your cell phone password, any necessary social media account passwords, and a list of individuals you want to be contacted. Make sure their phone numbers and email addresses are also provided.

Here are two situations I experienced that highlight the importance of timely notifications and contact lists. I had an amazing conversation with Bob, a former client/colleague on a recent Labor Day weekend. We talked for about an hour and agreed to talk again the following year around Labor Day weekend.

I realized in September that it was time for our conversation. I sent Bob a text. About a month later, I came across that text and then sent him another, "Hey, let's get our annual conversation scheduled." And then I thought, "Uh Oh." He had mentioned some recent health problems that had been brought under control. I googled his name, state, and the word "obituary" and his obituary came up. I was so sad that he was gone, and I didn't know. Leaving a list of your friends to contact out of state is a lovely idea to keep people informed.

Following my mother's service, I went through her address book and email list and depending on the relationship, sent them a note or an email, telling them of her passing. My mother had a friend that went quiet in the days before search engines and was so upset that she couldn't find out what had happened to her friend. Leaving a list of your friends, their contact information, and your preferred method of contacting them shows kindness to your family as they share the news and to your friends as they receive the news.

Important Information and Documents

Do you have a trust? If so, who has it? Where is it located? Is there a transfer upon death for the trust? Your family will need to know where to find it as well as other important information and documents including:

- Will/trust
- Real estate/car deeds and title insurance
- Bank account passwords
- Retirement records and pension contact information
- Stock and 401(k) information
- Safety deposit box information
- Safe combination
- Phone password
- Social media account logins and passwords
- Funeral policies
- Cemetery property deeds

From personal experience, I just happened to look at my mother's email one more time and noticed a notification from a bank. I was unaware of an account at that bank. There was a balance of $5,000 that would have been lost. Several of her accounts required two-party identification and since we had turned off her cell phone, that led to some additional issues. While this information doesn't have to be included in your funeral plan, if it isn't, it should include some pointers to where all the important documents are located.

Body or Organ Donation

An option that is very appealing to some people is body or organ donation. The requirements for body donation depend on a number of factors. Who is the "local" access that would be receiving bodies for body donation? It is usually a teaching hospital. There are a variety of processes that might apply depending on the institution that is receiving the body. It is important to review the post use of the body, because the body is typically cremated and the ashes could be returned to you or disposed of per their policy. There might be a process to be pre-approved to be in the body donation program. If so, there would need to be communication with that institution ahead of time. Even if there is pre-approval for body donation, there could be some determining factors at the time of death, that would prevent participation in the program. That may or may not include any communicable disease or weight. While the institution accepting the body may not charge a fee, the funeral home that arranges the initial transport and files the death certificate paperwork usually charges a fee.

Anyone can sign up to be an organ donor through their state. However, the process and programs for participating hospitals in an organ donation network can be very different. It's very important to communicate to a family member that you want to be an organ donor. Even if you have an organ donor designation on your driver's license, the hospital or organ transplant network will contact your next of kin to get permission. Donations might include major organs, but could also include eyes, bones, and/or tissue.

There are health conditions that prevent someone from being an organ donor like cancer, heart disease, or a rapidly spreading infection. There are other situations where there might be a plan with a medical teaching university to donate organs for further study, as in a brain donation. Organ donations don't prevent the ability to have a viewing or a traditional casketed funeral. There are still funeral home costs for transport and paperwork, but they could be reduced.

I Love You Club

I recently heard about a group of men that decided to gather and put detailed information together for their family. They gather every week or so with one task to complete each week. For example, one week a task is to gather each financial product and put it in one place with account numbers and passwords. The next meeting might be to discuss funeral wishes, wills, or trusts. By gathering with friends to do these activities, it provides accountability, camaraderie, and transparency as this information is gathered for when an event requires it. Turning something that could be mundane into something that could be considered fun and easier to do with friends over coffee or a drink is a great idea. One of the spouses came up with the name of the club because they're doing this work ahead of need, so it'll be easier on their loved ones.

Estate Lawyers and Trust Attorneys

Instead of gathering with your friends you could engage with an estate lawyer or trust attorney to make sure the documents needed have been identified and perhaps rolled into a trust for ease of execution at the time of need. That can be a hard step to take, but so important in terms of identifying assets and perhaps making good decisions for tax purposes.

A word about power of attorney (POA) and durable power of attorney (DPOA) requirements. If you're serving as a DPOA for a person or family member, it's important to include language in the DPOA that you have permission in the POA/DPOA to make funeral decisions for the person in which you're serving in that role. A POA/DPOA typically ends at death, so that language is critical if you're extending those responsibilities to that person or entity.

An estate lawyer I knew told every client that they need three things in place:
- Medical power of attorney
- Financial trust
- Funeral plan

As he met with his clients, the younger ones, typically in their fifties, would put together the first two items but then leave off the third.

One Monday morning, the estate lawyer heard of the passing of one of his clients. About noon, he gets a phone call from the husband of the client who passed, and the spouse told the estate lawyer that he was mad at him. The estate lawyer responded with, "I'm sorry about Mary passing, but why are you mad at me?"

His response was, "You told us to get a funeral plan in place, but you didn't make us. Now, I am meeting with a funeral director in two hours, and I have no idea what or how to plan the funeral or what she would have wanted." A good estate or trust lawyer will have this on their list to make sure their clients have their wishes identified.

Veterans

"Our debt to the heroic men and valiant women in the service of our country can never be repaid. They have earned our undying gratitude." —Harry S. Truman

If you're a veteran, you have some additional items to consider. Do you want military honors? If so, at the church or gravesite? Would you like to be buried in a military cemetery? The interest in military honors and recognition can vary between veterans. Some want no recognition, and some want all available honors. There are different honors depending on retirement from the military or service with an honorable discharge.

Please communicate your decisions to your family. Every veteran can receive a flag in honor of their service, and you can be buried at no charge, in a military cemetery. There are other benefits as well.

To schedule military honors, you need discharge papers called the DD214. All service members understand how important the DD214 is; however it may have been a long time since their service ended and it may be difficult to locate. Information from the Veterans Administration (VA) website is important to access for the most current information.

All information regarding eligibility can be found on the Veterans Administration website. This includes who's eligible for burial in a VA national cemetery Veterans, service members, spouses, and dependents may be eligible for burial in a VA national cemetery as well as receiving other benefits, if they meet at least one of these requirements:

- The person qualifying for burial benefits is a Veteran who didn't receive a dishonorable discharge, or
- The person qualifying for burial benefits is a service member who died while on active duty, active duty for training, or inactive duty for training, or
- The person qualifying for burial benefits is the spouse or surviving spouse of a Veteran (even if they remarried after the Veteran's death), or
- The person qualifying for burial benefits is the minor child of a Veteran (even if the Veteran died first) or, in some cases, the unmarried adult dependent child of a Veteran.

VA Memorial Benefits

The Veterans Administration (VA) takes special care to pay lasting tribute to the memory of veterans who served and sacrificed and that of their families. VA meticulously maintains 155 VA national cemeteries in 44 states and Puerto Rico and is working to increase access to accommodate veterans and eligible family members close to home. Currently, more than 94% of Veterans have a burial option in an open VA, state or tribal veterans' cemetery located within 75 miles of their home.

Note that most if not all these benefits may be provided for veterans who are buried in a state, territory, or tribal veterans cemetery. Check with the cemetery to ensure coverage. Some benefits are also available for veterans who choose burial in a private cemetery.

Veterans with a qualifying discharge are entitled to VA burial benefits. Spouses and dependent children are eligible too, even if they predecease the veteran.

Burial in a VA national cemetery includes these burial benefits:
- Opening and closing of the grave for burial of casketed or cremated remains, or placement of cremated remains in an above-ground vault, also called a columbarium
- A government furnished grave liner
- Perpetual care of the gravesite
- A headstone or marker with an inscription
- A burial flag
- A Presidential Memorial Certificate
- Some survivors may also be entitled to VA burial allowances as partial reimbursement for the costs of funerals and burials for eligible veterans

Note: Military honors can be granted at the national cemetery, at a private cemetery, church, or funeral home.

Gravesites in a VA national cemetery cannot be reserved. To prepare for a private cemetery burial, VA suggests families review a series of questions and complete required forms in advance. To access this information, go to www.va.gov.

What are your thoughts on ...

Write this down for your family:
Death certificate information:

Family and friends contact information:

Location of important information and documents:

If you are interested in organ donation, research local transplant organization coordination and what is required for advanced notification of your donation request.

Names and contact information for estate lawyers and/or trust attorneys:

If a veteran, please identify where DD214 information is stored, which is a required document for military honor or burial in a national cemetery:

"I do not fear death. I had been dead for billions and billions of years before I was born and had not suffered the slightest inconvenience from it."

—Mark Twain

CHAPTER 10
What Happens at the End?

Take Your Time

When a death occurs, take your time. It's important to not feel rushed. Pause and be still in these moments. Perhaps there's a comfort that any suffering has given way to peace. If your family member has chosen cremation, this could be the last time that you'll see them. Again, take your time. Some families want to do the hair or makeup of their loved one. Those simple acts can bring comfort in the most difficult of moments of loss.

Who to Call

We reviewed earlier what happens when someone dies suddenly in the home or who is not under hospice care. In a situation where you have been with your loved one, when they pass, the hospice firm or hospital will call the funeral home. There are certain pieces of information that they need to provide to the funeral home including:

- Name of the decedent
- Date and time of death
- Address for the transport team
- Name of doctor who will sign the death certificate

This assures the funeral home that the person was under medical care and there are no details that require additional investigation.

Hopefully, because of your thoughtful planning, you know who to call or refer to the hospital or hospice firm. You researched and made decisions. Even if you think you're twenty-five years away from needing help for you or a family member, you've checked out pricing and location and reputation and consulted friends who have needed funeral assistance in the recent past and you know who to call.

Expense Estimates

Now that you understand each aspect of your funeral, it's time to identify an estimate of the expenses. There's quite a difference between cremation and traditional funeral expenses.

- Do you want to include a budget for a reception or celebration of life?
- Will you provide honorariums for the service participants?
- Would you like to leave money to the church?
- Would you like to include money for out-of-state children and grandchildren to travel to the funeral?

It's best to budget for your funeral expenses and put that money in your own identified financial product. It will grow faster there than it will with the funeral home in an insurance or trust product. If you think there will be a need to go on Medicaid in the future, you can anticipate and pre-pay your funeral expenses, to meet the requirements of that path. It's wise to go ahead and purchase cemetery property. If you can, pay the open and close expenses sooner rather than later. You can even go ahead and pre-pay and place the marker. It can be updated with date of death after. Those are all very personal decisions and arrangements that your family will appreciate you having in place.

Pre-paid funeral plans involve making arrangements and payments in advance for one's own funeral expenses. It's a contractual agreement between an individual and a funeral service provider using prices that cannot increase over time. With a pre-paid funeral plan, you choose and pay for the funeral services and products in advance, including the casket, funeral ceremony, burial plot, cremation, or other components of the funeral service.

The funds for prepaid arrangements are typically held in a trust or insurance policy until the time of need. You can research which option is best for you. Just because you've purchased a pre-paid funeral plan with a funeral home doesn't mean you have to use that firm. You may have pre-paid and moved to another city or state. That money paid to a funeral home or pre-paid plan is your money. The funeral home in the city where you purchased it may be the beneficiary, but it's your money, and the beneficiary can be moved. If you've pre-paid for a traditional funeral and you change your mind to cremation, that money should be able to be refunded to you, if you are not on Medicaid. If you travel internationally regularly, you might consider an insurance policy for re-patriating the body back to your home city. Cremation and even traditional body preparation can be expensive in foreign countries with long wait times. This could provide you the peace of mind that if the worst thing could happen, you have the answers for your family to put into place.

By budgeting the dollar amount, in today's dollars, depending on what type of financial vehicle you put it in, your money in your financial product might grow faster than the costs of the funeral home. By itemizing this total, you can be comfortable that you have an approximation of the costs and a place that is holding the money for your family. If you would like to pre-pay the funeral, a funeral home can assist you. It's helpful to ask what kind of financial vehicle they use? Also, if you're out of town and you pass, how does it work to transfer the funds to an out-of-town funeral home?

In Closing
"I can't think of a more wonderful thanksgiving for the life I have had than that everyone should be jolly at my funeral."
—*Admiral Lord Mountbatten*

As a reminder we don't want to go, and no one wants you to go. It's important to do this planning exercise if you're ill, but it will be so much easier if you're not.

Everyone has hope and wants you to have hope, but after you have a serious illness, it's too hard to bring up the topic of funeral wishes. It's much easier to do with friends, over a cup of coffee or glass of wine, before there's a situation around this topic. *Before You Go* helps highlight your preferences when the unthinkable happens. You've left guidance about what's important to you, how to memorialize and celebrate your life. You've left family and friends with the gift of peace and confidence by outlining your wishes.

Leaving Guidance
Leaving guidance for your family isn't only about leaving the information for the service details. It's about leaving your personal preferences. They want to know that this is what you wanted. Every piece of information can give them confidence that they're making the best decision for you and settle any difference of opinions among family members.

With that in mind, it's the perfect time to capture some of your important philosophies on life. Maybe some of your favorite memories. Recently, I was with my sons and the picture they had of me and my goals when I was in college was very different than who I was in college. They saw me as someone who has always had it all together. That was certainly not the way I saw myself and truly not the way it all began. I told them, "I think my story is one of perseverance." What do you want your family to know about you?

As you look more in depth, you can expound on several areas.
- What accomplishment do you feel good about?
- What are some of your fondest memories?
- What people have had the greatest impact on your life?
- What things would you like to do before you die?
- If you could live your life over again, what would you spend more time doing? What would you spend less time doing?
- What behaviors and attitudes do you admire in others?
- What causes and beliefs are you most passionate about?
- What's the most fun you've ever had?
- I have a friend who insists we include what I promise not to do when I get old, and, apologizing in advance to my children for anything I might do.

We typically only plan funerals for family members and make these decisions perhaps two-three times in our lifetime, which makes it difficult to be a wise consumer. There might be twenty years between planning each parents' funeral. That makes it difficult to recall the details of those decisions.

You've just finished reading this book, and your head is swimming with ideas. You're probably wondering, where do I begin?

As you review your thoughts in each chapter, it's the perfect time to remember that you are leaving these thoughts, suggestions and instructions to give your family peace. As you capture how you would like your life celebrated, be sure and tell your spouse, child and/or best friend that you have written down your wishes in this book! On the worst day, if you have shared with them that you have documented your wishes and have told someone where the book is located, they will be able to find it and make plans accordingly. As they review the additional information that you have detailed in *Before You Go*, they have all that they need to create a remembrance event. Likewise, if you work with your family members and if they have documented their wishes, you have all of the information and then confidence that you are fulfilling their wishes. To leave this information behind is an act of love.

Citations:

- *https://www.ibisworld.com/united-states/market-research-reports/coffin-casket-manufacturing-industry/#IndustryStatisticsAndTrends*
- *www.returnhome.com*
- *https://www.ibisworld.com/united-states/market-research-reports/coffin-casket-manufacturing-industry/#IndustryStatisticsAndTrends*
- *CANA Cremation Association of North America*
- *Empathy.com*
- *Funeral Wise*
- *www.choose.va.gov*
- *www.HomeFuneral.org.uk*
- *www.choose.va.gov*
- *www.PerfectMemorials.com*
- *www.choose.va.gov*
- *www.trigard.com*
- *www.TulipCremation.com*
- *www.returnhome.com*

What are your thoughts on ...

Funeral budget?

If I have set aside funds for my funeral, where can my family find them?

I have included funds for travel for relatives and if so which relatives?

I have included funds for a party and receptions.

What are your thoughts on ...

Fondest memories?

Accomplishments that you are most proud of?

What behaviors and attitudes do you admire in others?

What causes and beliefs are you most passionate about?

GLOSSARY

Aftercare
Services and support provided to bereaved families after the funeral, including grief counseling and support groups.

Ashes
The cremated remains of a deceased person, also known as cremains.

Burial
The act of placing a deceased person's body into the ground, typically in a casket within a grave.

Burial Ground
A designated area where deceased individuals are buried. This term is often used interchangeably with cemetery but can also refer to less formal or historical burial sites.

Casket
A box or chest for burying a deceased person, usually made of wood, metal, or other materials.

Cemetery
A designated area of land for burying the dead.

Cemetery Plot
A specific piece of land within a cemetery where a casket is buried.

Coach
A vehicle specifically designed to transport the deceased from the funeral home to the cemetery.

Columbarium
A structure with niches or spaces to hold urns containing cremated remains. Often found in cemeteries or mausoleums.

Cremation
The process of reducing a deceased body to ashes through intense heat.

Crematorium
A facility where cremation is performed.

Direct Burial
A burial without a preceding funeral or memorial service.

Direct Cremation
A cremation without a preceding funeral or memorial service.

Embalming
The process of preserving a deceased body by using chemicals to delay decomposition.

Eulogy
A speech or written tribute honoring a deceased person, typically delivered at a funeral service.

Funeral
A ceremony marking a person's death, often involving rituals, religious practices, and a gathering of family and friends.

Funeral Director
A professional who manages funeral services, including the preparation of the deceased, organizing the funeral, and assisting the family.

Funeral Home

A business that provides funeral services, including preparation of the body, conducting ceremonies, and offering cremation or burial options.

Funeral Rule

The Funeral Rule, enforced by the Federal Trade Commission, requires funeral directors to give you itemized prices in person and, if you ask, over the phone. The rule also requires funeral directors to give you other information about their goods and services. For example, if you ask about funeral arrangements in person, the funeral home must give you a written price list to keep that shows the goods and services the home offers. If you want to buy a coffin or outer burial container, the funeral provider must show you descriptions of the available selections and the prices before actually showing you the coffins.

Many funeral providers offer various packages of commonly selected goods and services that make up a funeral. But when you arrange for a funeral, you have the right to buy individual goods and services. That is, you do not have to accept a package that may include items you do not want.

According to the Funeral Rule:
- You have the right to choose the funeral goods and services you want (with some exceptions).
- The funeral provider must state this right in writing on the general price list.
- If state or local law requires you to buy any particular item, the funeral provider must disclose it on the price list, with a reference to the specific law.
- The funeral provider may not refuse, or charge a fee, to handle a coffin you bought elsewhere.
- A funeral provider that offers cremations must make alternative containers available.

Grave
A place of burial for a deceased person, usually a hole dug in the ground.

Grave Marker
A headstone or plaque placed at the head of a grave, identifying the deceased person buried there.

Graveside Service
A funeral service held at the cemetery, typically at the site of the grave.

Headstone
A stone slab or marker placed at the head of a grave, typically engraved with the deceased's name, birth and death dates, and sometimes an epitaph or artwork.

Hearse
A vehicle specifically designed to transport the deceased from the funeral home to the cemetery.

Interment
The act of placing a deceased person into a grave or tomb.

Mausoleum
A building designed to house the remains of the deceased above ground, often containing crypts or niches.

Memorial Service
A ceremony honoring the deceased, usually held without the body present.

Monument
A structure, statue, or plaque erected to commemorate a person or event. In cemeteries, monuments often mark graves or family plots.

Niche
A compartment within a columbarium, mausoleum, or wall, designed to hold an urn containing cremated remains.

Obituary
A notice of a person's death, often including a brief biography and details about the funeral or memorial service.

Pallbearer
A person who helps carry the casket during a funeral service.

Perpetual Care
A fund established to maintain the grounds, structures, and landscape of a cemetery indefinitely. It ensures that the cemetery remains in good condition over time.

Plot
A specific piece of land within a cemetery where a person or family is buried. Plots can be sold as single, double, or family plots.

Repatriation
The process of returning a deceased person's body to their home country or place of origin.

Sexton
An official responsible for the maintenance of a churchyard or cemetery, including the digging of graves.

Tomb
A structure or chamber where a deceased person is buried. Tombs can be located above or below ground and are often marked with inscriptions or monuments.

Urn
A container used to hold the cremated remains of a deceased person.

Vault

A sealed container that is placed in the ground to encase a casket. Vaults are used to protect the casket and prevent the ground from settling.

Viewing

A scheduled time for family and friends to see the deceased person, typically held at a funeral home before the funeral service.

Visitation

A scheduled time for friends and family to view the deceased and offer condolences to the family.

Wake

A gathering of family and friends before the funeral, often involving a viewing of the deceased and held to honor and remember the deceased.

After the passing of a close family member, Cathy Boomer came to understand the importance of compassion and care during those early moments of grief and loss.

That personal journey would inform and inspire a new professional chapter. Cathy created her vision of a small, comforting, trustworthy licensed funeral home to thoughtfully care for families.

Drawing from her exceptional interpersonal skills developed during her award-winning computer sales career and her abiding passion for service, Cathy focused on bringing a paradigm-shift in the funeral industry in Kansas City. After extensive research and training, she then founded Signature Funerals to offer families an additional choice for their funeral care in Kansas City. Her approach blends traditional values with innovative, modern options. This gives each person permission to create meaningful, lasting memories that are unique for each family. She considers it an honor to care for your loved ones during this time of loss.

A Kansas City native and University of Kansas alumna, Cathy and her team at Signature Funerals have provided cremation and traditional funeral services to the Kansas City area, for over 15 years. She has been married for over 40 years and she and her husband are the proud parents of 4 children, including an Air Force officer, two daughters-in-law and three granddaughters.

A tireless volunteer in her community, Cathy enjoys memberships in her church and several professional and philanthropic organizations.